Walking in the Clwydian Range

Following Offa's Dyke Path over Penycloddiau

Walking in the
Clwydian Range

Twenty one circular walks in and around the
Clwydian Range Area of Outstanding Natural Beauty

Carl Rogers

MARA BOOKS

First published in March 2002 by **Mara Books**,
22 Crosland Terrace, Helsby, Frodsham, Cheshire WA6 9LY.
Second edition published December 2006.

All enquiries regarding sales telephone: (01928) 723744

TEN DIGIT – ISBN 1 902512 14 6
THIRTEEN DIGIT – ISBN 978 1 902512 14 3

Thanks to Bob Nash for checking route descriptions and Lorna
Jenner for writing the 'Flora and fauna' section. Thanks also to
Alan Roe for the use of his photograph of Rhuddlan Castle on
page 18.

Contents

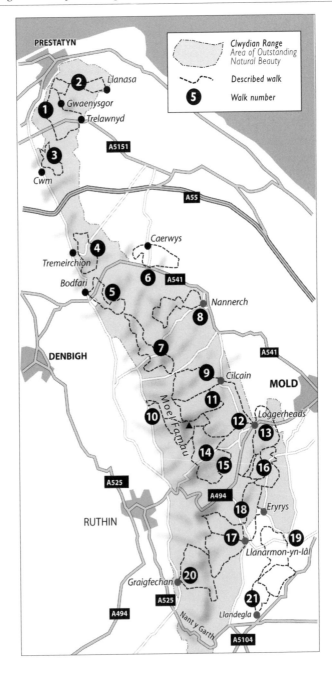

PRESTATYN

Clwydian Range
Area of Outstanding
Natural Beauty

Described walk

5 Walk number

Llanasa

Gwaenysgor

Trelawnyd

A5151

Cwm

A55

Caerwys

Tremeirchion

Bodfari

Nannerch

DENBIGH

Cilcain

MOLD

Loggerheads

Moel Famau

Eryrys

A525

RUTHIN

Llanarmon-yn-Iâl

Graigfechan

A525

A494

Nant y Garth

Llandegla

A5104

Introduction

THE CLWYDIAN RANGE IS ONE OF THE MOST distinctive hill groups in the Welsh borders. Dividing the broad valleys of the Dee and the Clwyd, they run north-south for almost 18 miles rising just north of the Nant-y-Garth Pass near Llandegla and almost tumbling into the sea at Prestatyn. They are at their most impressive when viewed from the west across the flat low lying meadows of the Vale of Clwyd, where they present an unbroken wall of striking hills filling the skyline. They will be remembered by many walkers for providing either a fitting climax or a rigorous introduction to the Offa's Dyke Path National Trail, which runs the entire length of the Welsh border.

Moel Arthur from the Vale of Clwyd

The Clwydian Range viewed from the west beyond Ruthin

In 1985 the unique character of this area was recognised when it became one of Wales' five Areas of Outstanding Natural Beauty (AONB). The AONB boundary takes in the entire Clwydian Range from the Nant-y-Garth Pass in the south, to the limestone escarpments above Prestatyn in the north. To the west it is defined by the Vale of Clwyd and extends east beyond Afon Alyn to include the limestone plateau of Nercwys Mountain.

Within this area there is great diversity, defined mainly by the underlying geology. The dominant feature is of course the ridge itself, composed mainly of ancient Silurian shales and mudstones interbedded with bands of sandstone. The resulting outlines are soft though often quite striking—Moel Arthur, Foel Fenlli and Moel Gyw are fine examples. Outcrops are almost nonexistent, but the higher hills such as Moel Famau and Moel

Gyw have dramatic sweeping cwms on their eastern faces which may well be glacial in origin. Outcrops of limestone occur mainly to the east of Afon Alyn and on the lower hills to the north.

The western limit of the whole range is defined by the dramatic fall into the Vale of Clwyd—the eroded wall of an ancient rift valley. Long 'V' shaped valleys running down from the main ridge are a prominent feature of these sunny western slopes, whilst much of the high ground is clad in open heather moorland. This is now greatly reduced compared to earlier centuries and is under constant threat from agricultural 'improvement' or afforestation, such as can be seen at Moel Famau. The lesser tops have mostly been cultivated and enclosed to form large grazing fields.

The nearest neighbouring hills lie to the west beyond the Vale of Clwyd and south across the Llandegla Moors—the distance

Stunning winter conditions on Foel Fenlli

giving height and stature to summits which never reach 2,000 feet (Moel Famau is the highest point at 1,817 feet, 554 metres). Views can be breathtaking in clear conditions reaching west across the Denbigh Moors to the mountains of Snowdonia and southwest along the Llantysilio ridge to the Berwyn hills. To the east the view stretches across the Cheshire Plain to the Pennines and in exceptional conditions north across the Irish Sea to the mountains of Cumbria and the Isle of Man.

Many sections of the ridge are justifiably popular and are thus well walked—Moel Famau Country Park is a favourite picnic and outdoor venue, whilst the Offa's Dyke Path traverses the entire range. However, even the most popular tops have lesser known approaches and where possible it is these paths which the following walks seek out.

The northern end of the AONB, beyond the Wheeler gap sees a change to carboniferous limestone as the dominant bedrock.

Here the hills gradually lose height to merge with the green fields of the Trelawnyd plateau. More intensively cultivated, walks in this area are most often through farmland, woods and along old green lanes, although there are still hills and views on the northern and western edges of the plateau.

To the east of Afon Alyn is another band of carboniferous limestone—the river marking the approximate divide with the Silurian rocks of the main ridge. Instead of the soft outlines of the Silurian rocks, craggy terraced escarpments and plateauland—more reminiscent of Yorkshire than Wales—are found. The occasional craggy hilltop gives superb views of the Clwydian ridge across the Alyn valley and one or two large deciduous woods make a welcome change from the conifer plantations found elsewhere.

The search for lead and more recently the quarrying of limestone for use in road building has had quite an impact on this area and quarrying activities, as well the remains of lead mining, are much in evidence although often surprisingly well hidden. Nevertheless, you will no doubt be surprised at the size and scale of some of the modern quarrying operations, whilst the remains of lead mining are quietly being reclaimed by nature.

Most of the walks can be enjoyed at all times of the year, each season having its own charm, but outside of the summer months be prepared for cold and wet conditions. Wet grass and mud will be encountered on nearly all the walks to varying degrees, while occasional Arctic-like conditions can be experienced on the higher tops during a cold snap. Equip yourself with these conditions in mind and you will enjoy your walking.

Finally, the area has many villages with superb old traditional pubs where you can reward yourself at the end of your walk!

History

THE HISTORY OF THE AREA reaches way back into the depths of prehistory with most periods of settlement represented, although the very earliest Neolithic remains are confined mainly to the northern end of the range near the coast—notably the large stone cairn at Gop Hill near Trelawnyd. The earliest settlers arrived by sea and seem to have remained in coastal areas, rarely penetrating inland where thick woodland and swamps in the lower valleys would have made travel extremely difficult. Only gradually would the interior have been opened up by settlers.

By the Bronze Age things were different. Forest clearance continued and finds throughout the range suggest greater access to the interior, particularly along the hills.

Towards the end of this period, around 500 BC, Iron Age tribes entered Britain from the continent. They seem to have brought with them a more restless and warlike culture and their most

Moel y Gaer, an Iron Age hillfort on the western flanks of Moel Famau

notable legacy is the many hillforts whose earthworks remain for us to ponder, over 2,000 years later. The hilly landscape of the Clwydian Range seems to have been ideal for the Celts and at least six hill forts are found encircling summits in the range, with the best examples to be found at Penycloddiau, Moel y Gaer and Foel Fenlli. The use of earlier sites originally occupied during the Bronze Age is suggested by a hoard of bronze axes found at Moel Arthur.

The Celts were organised into tribes with the Deceangli occupying this part of northeast Wales, the Venedotae to the west, the Ordovices to the south and the Cornovii to the east in what is now Cheshire and Shropshire. It was these people who faced the Roman invasion in the first century.

Although the Romans left few remains in our area, their influence must soon have been felt here with one of the main fortresses in western Britain almost within sight at what is now Chester (Deva). From the ramparts of the hillfort on Penycloddiau, the sails of Roman galley ships would have been visible entering and leaving the port by the long arm of the River Dee. By 61 AD the Romans had crossed these hills and pushed into the remote west having crushed a rebellion of the Druids on Anglesey. Their main fortress in North Wales was established at Caernarfon (Segontium) and the road which linked Segontium to Deva passed through the gap in the hills used today by the modern A55 at Rhuallt.

Under Roman rule Britain was to remain relatively peaceful for almost 300 years, but when the Romans withdrew they left behind a political vacuum. The kingdom lay undefended and suffered attacks from all sides. The earliest of these came from the Irish who began to invade the west coast and established colonies throughout Wales.

In response to this, a powerful chieftain or ruler from Manaw Gododdin (a northern British kingdom soon to disappear), either came or was sent to what is now North Wales in a bid to expel the invaders. His name was Cunedda and he created a large kingdom for himself which he ruled from Aberffraw on Anglesey. The dynasty he established ruled Gwynedd and much of North Wales until the time of Edward I. The Clwydian Range seems to have marked the eastern limit of Gwynedd with the land to the east under the control of the kingdom which would later become Powys. This may have been centred on the old Roman city of Chester and would have included much of what is now Cheshire up to the edge of the Pennines.

It was about this time that Christianity is thought to have arrived in western Britain from Ireland. Travelling preachers set up *'llans'*—circular enclosures containing the preachers' cell. These became local centres of worship and eventually settlements developed around them. Many village dedications date from this period and most frequently carry the name of the founder e.g. Llandegla—originated as the *llan* of Saint Tegla.

Unfortunately Cunedda's success with the Irish was not repeated in eastern Britain where Germanic tribes were harassing the east coast and Picts from beyond Hadrian's Wall were making raids into what is now northern England. The king of Britain at the time was the enigmatic character known as Vortigern. Few details are known about him for sure, but he is generally blamed for initiating the Saxon colonisation of England in the late fifth century. In an attempt to control the attacks on his kingdom he is said to have enlisted the help of Saxon mercenaries from the Continent. At first this was successful, but the Saxons soon turned on their employer, took lands for themselves and began establishing their own kingdoms. This led to fierce conflict with the British, but the Saxon colonisation—unlike that of the Irish—could not be stopped. The whole of eastern Britain soon came under their control and by the seventh century, the British tribes who survived were confined mainly to the north and west of Britain.

From this time on the British were under constant threat from the Saxons and their desperate need for a hero who would deliver them from their enemies is woven into the myths and legends surrounding the character of King Arthur. They did, however, have one or two notable successes against the invaders and one—known as the 'Alleluia Victory'—is reputed to have occurred close to Mold and is remembered in the dedication of the church at Llanarmon yn Iâl.

The British were led to victory by Germanus, Bishop of Auxerre who, like many of his associates, added politics to his duties as spiritual leader. As a result, when an army of heathen Saxons threatened North Wales, he quickly mustered a 'Christian' British force to oppose them. When the armies met near Mold at what has come to be known as 'Garmon's Field', the British are said to have advanced shouting "Alleluia" (praise Jah or God). For some reason this is said to have terrified the heathens so

A monument to the Alleluia Victory at Maesgarmon near Mold

much that they all turned and ran without a blow being struck. Many died in the nearby river, the rest being put to the sword by the triumphant Welsh as they fled, resulting in what was believed to be a miraculous victory. A monument near Mold with a date of 420 AD commemorates the battle .

Two centuries later however, the Saxons were to have their revenge when the roles were very much reversed. An army from one of the most powerful Saxon kingdoms, Northumbria, pushed west and drove a wedge between the British of northern and western Britain. This took the form of a great victory on the banks of the River Dee in 616 AD between Chester and Bangor-is-y-coed near Wrexham. The leader of the army was Aethelfrith and the British army he faced had only partly gathered when the fighting began. From the nearby abbey came over 1,000 monks to pray for a victory over the heathens, but their prayers went unheard. Many would have been retired warriors themselves, but unarmed they were cut down like corn by the axe-wielding Saxons. Among the slain were many members of the royal house of Powys.

This victory effectively severed the British—who occupied what is now Wales—from their kinsmen in what would become northern England and Cornwall, confining them to the land that we know today as Wales. From this time on, they developed as a separate people and began to call themselves 'Cymry' or 'fellow countrymen'. Ironically their new neighbours—who soon colonised adjacent Cheshire and the city of Chester—called them 'wealas' or foreigners from which we get the name Wales/Welsh. The division between the Cymry and the Saxons was dictated mainly by geography and lay approximately on the line of the present border of Wales, but this border was never static and the lands to either side were constantly overrun. Here in the north the Clwydian Range lay within this frontier territory and saw little peace for the next 600 years.

Unlike the Romans, the Saxons were unable to completely conquer the Welsh who entrenched themselves beyond the mountains of the west and rarely faced their enemies in open battles which they knew they could not win. While they remained in the hills and mountains they were safe. There were however, periods of complicated power struggles when Welsh leaders and Princes allied themselves with one Saxon kingdom against a neighbour, often their own countrymen. To contain the Welsh, Offa, the eighth century king of Mercia (a kingdom which occupied much of central England including Cheshire, Shropshire and southern Lancashire), satisfied himself by confining the Welsh to the highland region in the west with his great earthwork a few miles to the west of the present Welsh border. The dyke disappears north of Treuddyn near Wrexham, so Offa's frontier is unclear here in the north. He died in battle at Rhuddlan in 796 AD.

Others would follow Offa in a quest for territory in the west— the rich lands of the Vale of Clwyd were a much sought after prize and one well worth fighting for. As a result it was constantly invaded, captured, lost and re-captured again—one reason for the 'Englishness' of northeast Wales today, although it never became English and English place names are still in the minority.

When the Saxon king Harold fell on the field at Hastings in 1066 the event may have seemed insignificant and remote to Wales, but the effect of this defeat would soon be felt all along the borderlands. Within a matter of months a new menace presented itself beyond the dyke. The Normans were the most organised and powerful fighting forced of their day and they were not content to let an unconquered nation live untouched beyond Offa's Dyke. William tackled the problem by giving lands along the border to powerful and ambitious barons with a free reign to attack and plunder adjacent Welsh kingdoms in order to increase their own lands and power. They became known as 'Marcher Lords' and caused the Welsh endless trouble during the early Middle Ages. There were three strategic centres along the border: Hereford, Shrewsbury and Chester.

William installed Hugh of Avranches, known as 'Hugh Lupus',

at Chester with the task of opening up lands in North Wales. Hugh's second in command was Robert of Rhuddlan who proved to be very ambitious and was soon pushing west to Afon Clwyd where he built a fortress at Rhuddlan on the site of an early Welsh fort. This coincided with civil war in Gwynedd which he was able to exploit and established himself as far west as Deganwy. Here he tried to claim Gwynedd for himself but he was far from the protection of his lord and was killed defending the castle against the Welsh.

The Clwydian Range provided an obstacle to these invasions but the Romans had built a good road between Deva (Chester) and Segontium (Caernarfon) enabling armies to move quickly

Edward I's castle at Rhuddlan

and easily west into Welsh lands. Chester thus made an ideal base and many English kings launched their campaigns from there throughout the Middle Ages. The Welsh still refer to Chester as Y Gaer—meaning *'the fort'*.

The Welsh were also active on their frontier and the English were pushed back from time to time. They built castles as far east as Ewloe and neighbouring castles fell into their hands many times.

The rise of Llywelyn Fawr and the prominence of his grandson Llywelyn ap Gruffydd ('Llywelyn the Last') led to Wales' final war with England in the thirteenth century. Edward I succeeded his father Henry III in 1277 and at his coronation he demanded the attendance of Prince Llywelyn to swear allegiance. When Llywelyn refused both to attend the coronation and swear allegiance to Edward, war broke out. Edward invaded North Wales from Chester and sent a fleet of ships to Anglesey to seize the crops on which the Welsh were so dependent. Llywelyn was cornered and compelled to surrender.

At the 'Treaty of Rhuddlan' Llywelyn lost most of his lands retaining only Snowdon and Anglesey. His brother Dafydd, who had fought for Edward against Llywelyn, was given rulership of the lands between the Conwy and the Dee. Ironically, it was Dafydd who triggered the final rebellion against Edward. He resented the interference of English officials left behind by the crown and called to his brother Llywelyn for help. Llywelyn answered the call and the two soon took control of the nearby castles at Harwarden, Ruthin and Hope. Support for the rising was great at first, but Edward was a powerful opponent and the chances of complete success were never great. The end came with Llywelyn's death in a minor skirmish near Builth Wells. Dafydd declared himself 'Prince of Wales' and continued the fight but was eventually handed over to the English by his own men. For side swopping Edward considered him a traitor and condemned him to death at Shrewsbury where he suffered a terrible execution, being publicly hung drawn and quartered in 1283.

Devil's Gorge, one of the lead mines in the limestone area east of Afon Alyn

Welsh independence was over. Edward built a ring of castles around North Wales to hold the kingdom in subjection and those at Flint and Rhuddlan still stand. The independent Welsh spirit was not crushed however; a century later one of the most famous of all Welsh rebel leaders was to rise—Owain Glyndŵr. He came from Glyn Dyfrdwy on the River Dee at the foot of the Llantysilio hills and was well into middle age when his rise to fame began.

The rebellion was triggered by a quarrel over a small piece of land with his neighbour, the English Lord Grey of Ruthin. When the king favoured Grey, Glyndŵr was declared an outlaw and responded by sacking Grey's estate at Ruthin. His countrymen rallied to his side and declared him 'Prince of Wales'. Support was great at first, even today he is remembered as one of the great national heroes of Wales, but his victory was short lived— little more than nine years and it was all over. He died in obscurity at an unknown location and passed into the folklore of the nation.

This brought an end to armed conflict between England and Wales, although the present boundary was not formalised for another century and a half with the Acts of Union in 1536 and 1542. Political stability brought greater prosperity to Wales and a number of lavishly endowed churches were built.

With the Acts of Union new markets were opened up in England and surplus cattle were taken over the mountains to be sold in the English Midlands. Many of the routes which were followed over the hills remain. Some have been formalised into roads and lanes, but many remain as quiet and often very picturesque footpaths and bridleways which are delight to walk.

Lead mining has been carried out in the limestone areas of northeast Wales on a small scale since the time of Edward I, but this increased dramatically during the Industrial Revolution, reaching a peak in the mid-nineteenth century. Facilities for smelting were available in the adjacent coalfields to the east where ironworks were already exploiting the rich supplies of coal needed for the furnaces. Villages like Maeshafn and Eryrys owe their origin to the search for lead and zinc in these hills and would have been very busy places when output was at its greatest. Populations swelled enormously and many existing cottages would have originated as ale houses, where the workers would have been relieved of their hard earned wages. Maeshafn has just one pub now but its name, 'The Miner's Arms', recalls its origins and the livelihoods of its first patrons.

In more recent times quarrying for stone to be used in road foundations has taken its toll with large workings at Graianrhyd, Maeshafn, Llanarmon-yn-Iâl and Cadole. There are still active workings within the area but expansion has been restricted and locals at Maeshafn were successful in saving a local beauty spot —Moel Findeg—from development.

Despite these activities much of the area remains unspoilt and the central section of the range has been a popular area for outdoor recreation since the 1920s when Crosville began a special Sunday bus from Liverpool to Loggerheads. The woods and gorges around Loggerheads gave many thousands from the urban areas of Merseyside and Deeside their first experience of the Welsh countryside. Crosville opened a cafe at Loggerheads and other visitor facilities developed nearby. Today a thriving visitor centre and country park managed by Denbighshire County Council operates from the site of the former bus stop and cafe.

Flora and fauna *by Lorna Jenner*

THE VARIED LANDSCAPE OF THE CLWYDIAN RANGE supports an equal variety of animal and plant life.

Heathland plants like heathers and bilberry thrive on the poor upland soils with bracken taking over in some areas and occasional wetter patches covered in mounds of red and green mosses, darker green rushes and tufts of cotton grass. Look for red grouse bursting out of the heather as you approach, buzzards wheeling overhead looking for their favoured prey of rabbits and, during the summer, many smaller migrants returning to breed on the moors.

The heather moorland is also home to the nationally scarce black grouse which has a stronghold on the slopes of Moel Famau. Denbighshire Countryside Service are managing the moorland to encourage grouse by selectively burning and cutting the heather, ensuring a mixture of fresh young shoots for food and woodier growth for shelter.

One very noticeable character is the perky little wheatear, who has usually arrived by April, often seen perching on a stone, flitting low over the ground or fluttering upwards to catch an insect. They call loudly and have an obvious white rump and black tail. The male in summer is particularly noticeable with his grey back with black cheeks and wings.

A completely different array of plants grow in the limestone areas such as Loggerheads. Colourful wildflowers thrive on these thin soils such as wild thyme, delicate quaking grass, deep pink cranesbill, yellow rock rose and an assortment of orchids. This array of flowers attracts many butterflies and other insects to feed on their nectar.

The fast flowing rivers and streams are also full of life. Look for dippers—small brown birds with a distinctive white chest — bobbing on riverside rocks or flying fast and low above the water or the more slender grey wagtails, with their yellow undersides

23

The damp woodland edging the Alyn is luxuriant with ferns and mosses

and long, constantly twitching tails. The river valleys of the Alyn and the Wheeler also provide good habitat for otters and watervoles.

Pockets of woodland break up the largely open landscape. The damp woodland edging the Alyn is luxuriant with ferns and mosses and the drier copses are dotted with primroses and violets in early spring and later carpeted with bluebells. The mature beech woodland near Maeshafn is particularly delightful, rich chestnut coloured in autumn, delicate green in late spring when the leaves are beginning to unfurl, or cool and shady in the summer, under the dappled canopy.

The conifer plantations too, though not as rich in wildlife as our native broadleaved woods, still provide food and shelter for many birds, animals and insects, particularly in the winter. Flocks of tits and finches are often seen flitting between branches and it is the favoured home of some species including coal tits, siskins and the tiny goldcrest.

Glossary of Welsh names

Afon	*river*	Hafod	*summer dwelling*
Allt	*hillside*	Hen	*old*
Bach/Fach	*little*	Isaf	*lower*
Bont/Pont	*bridge*	Llan	*church*
Bryn	*hill, eminence*	Llyn	*lake*
Cae	*field, enclosure*	Llys	*hall or court*
Caer/Gaer	*fort*	Lôn	*lane*
Canol	*centre*	Maen	*stone*
Capel	*chapel*	Môr	*sea*
Carreg	*crag or stone*	Mynach	*monk*
Castell	*castle*	Mynydd	*mountain*
Cefn	*ridge*	Newydd	*new*
Clwyd	*gate*	Ogof	*cave*
Coch/Goch	*red*	Pant	*hollow*
Coed	*wood*	Parc	*park*
Cors/Gors	*bog or swamp*	Pen	*head or point*
Craig/Graig	*crag*	Pentre	*village*
Croes/Groes	*cross*	Pistyll	*waterfall*
Cwm	*coombe*	Plas	*house*
Dinas	*city, fortress*	Pwll	*pool*
Ddu/Du	*black*	Rhos	*moorland*
Dŵr	*water*	Rhyd	*ford*
Dyffryn	*valley*	Sarn	*causeway*
Eglwys	*church*	Tomen	*mound*
Faes/Maes	*meadow*	Tref	*town*
Fawr/Mawr	*large*	Twll	*cavern*
Felin	*mill*	Twr	*tower*
Ffordd	*road*	Ty	*house*
Ffynnon	*well or fountain*	Tyddyn	*farmstead*
Foel/Moel	*bare hill*	Uchaf	*upper*
Garn	*an eminence*	Waun	*moorland*
Glas	*blue-green*	Wen	*white*
Glyn	*deep valley*	Y, Yr	*the*
Gwern/Wern	*alder coppice*	Yn	*in*
Gwyn	*white*	Ynys	*island*

Gwaenysgor & Gop Hill

Distance: *5¹/₂ miles*

A mainly gentle walk through farmland and along a section of the Offa's Dyke Path with broad views west along the coast to Snowdonia. An option to include a unique prehistoric mound is also included.

Start: Begin the walk from the triangular village green in the centre of Gwaenysgor where there is a small information board. *Grid ref: 075 811 (Landranger 116, Explorer 265).*

Gwaenysgor is an attractive unspoilt village with many fine old buildings. The information board sited on the green in the village centre gives details of the best examples. The unusual name is thought to mean 'the meadow of the camp', from gwaun—'meadow' and ysgor—'camp or fortification'. This could be a reference to the remains on Gop Hill or even to the northern limit of Offa's Dyke which may have ended somewhere near here. There is much controversy about exactly where the dyke finished or if it was ever completed after Offa's death in battle at Rhuddlan in 796 AD.

The walk

1. From the village centre head north along the Prestatyn road (towards masts on the hillside) and after about 75 yards turn left into an access road immediately before 'Brynffynnon'. At the end of the road and beyond the last house on the right, the lane continues as a footpath contained by hedges (ignore footpaths left and right by a stone well).

After a stile and kissing gate the path bends left under trees then between gorse bushes to eventually enter an open field. Go ahead through the field to reach the edge of the hillside overlooking Meliden and Prestatyn where you meet the Offa's Dyke Path. Cross the stile here and turn left along Offa's Dyke Path which follows the edge of the steep hillside with wide panoramas west along the coast.

Despite their modern appearance, both Meliden and Prestatyn are ancient settlements of Anglo-Saxon origin. They originate from a time of Saxon advance into Welsh lands, possibly during the seventh and eighth centuries, although this would always have been a dangerous frontier territory for those early settlers. Evidence for this can be seen in the nearby earthworks of Offa's Dyke and the earlier Watt's Dyke (both southeast of here) built to defend the border with Wales.

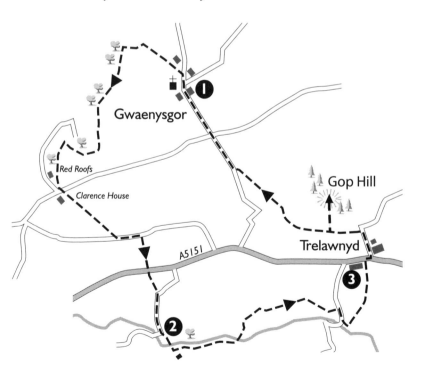

Following Offa's Dyke Path on the hills above Meliden

Meliden developed rapidly during the eighteenth century as a centre for lead mining and remains of this industry can still be seen nearby.

The name Prestatyn has been corrupted from a name similar to that of Preston in Lancashire and is evidence of the constant change in control of the area between the English and Welsh prior to Edward I's conquest. There are many other examples of Anglicised Welsh names and the Welsh spelling of names which are of Anglo-Saxon origin along the border which also originate from this period.

The modern form of Prestatyn came into being during the nineteenth century when the town developed as a tourist destination for the nearby industrial towns around Merseyside and Manchester. The coming of the railways in the mid-century brought North Wales within easy reach *of many thousands of trippers and a string of resorts developed all along this coast to cater for the new trade.*

Stay with the main path as it turns right down the slope to a junction. Keep left here on the Offa's Dyke Path ignoring the path to the right. Continue along the top of the hillside and eventually beside a fence overlooking a quarry on the right, finally entering woods. Keep right at a T junction here taking the signed path to 'Bryniau'.

At more open ground, keep left on the obvious path to eventually reach an access road with a house to the right ('Red Roofs'). Turn left up the driveway from the house to join a quiet lane. Turn left here, then left again at a T junction after a few yards. About 50 yards further on, look for a stile and sign on the right beside the driveway to 'Clarence House'.

Follow Offa's Dyke Path ahead through the following fields. This is well walked and supplied with stiles. After the final field a line of wooden steps takes you down the bank and into a lane. Turn left along the lane and after about 200 yards, turn right into fields again by a stile and sign. Walk up through the centre of a large field to a stile. Take a direct line through the following field to the road (A5151).

Cross the road, turn right and in about 50 yards go left on the signed path (ODP) almost opposite a large farm, to enter a lane once again. Turn right and walk along the lane until it bends very sharply to the right. Keep left here (straight ahead!) and follow an access road to a T junction with a large house on the left.

2. Take the left turn here (ODP bears right at this point). Follow the unmade road until it bears left to a house. Continue straight ahead here on the obvious footpath and a little further on ignore a path on the right keeping left to follow the sunken lane. A short section near the stream can be very wet but things soon improve.

At the next T junction (about ½ mile) turn right and continue to the lane. Turn right along the lane and just before the bend bear left onto a short section of old road before turning left onto a signed field path. Walk directly through a large field aiming for the top right-hand corner of the field where you will find a stile partly hidden in the hedge. In the following field, keep right along the hedge and after about 50 yards cross a stile on the right. Turn left now and continue on the opposite side of the hedge to join an access road near cottages.

3. Walk along the access road to the main road (A5151) in the centre of Trelawnyd. Turn right and after a few yards cross over taking the signed 'Llanasa' road ('High Street') on the left. Walk up the hill, but before the right-hand bend at the top of the rise, turn left into a short access road with a well hidden footpath sign. Beyond the final house a stone stile takes you into a large field on the lower slopes of Gop Hill. Contour the hillside keeping to the obvious footpath ahead. Partway along the path, a finger post indicates a permissive footpath to the summit of 'Bryn Gop' on the right. If you visit the summit return to this point to continue the walk.

Gop Hill is famous for the large prehistoric drystone cairn crowning its summit. This curious cone can be seen for several miles and is over 60 feet high making it the largest of its kind in Wales.

The view from the summit is extensive with the higher tops of Clwydian Range seen to the south across the green undulating fields of the Trelawnyd plateau. Wirral and the Lancashire coast can be seen to the east with the North Wales coast and Snowdonia out to the west.

At the far end of the field, keep right above farm buildings and a ruined stone dovecote quite close to the path on the left. Look for a stile in the corner of the field below woods on the right. Cross the stile and walk directly through the following field aiming just to the left of Gwaenysgor in the distance. Cross a stile in the far fence, then bear half-left to a second stile in the corner which leads into a lane. Turn right now and follow the lane back to Gwaenysgor keeping straight ahead at the crossroads.

Llanasa

Distance: *5¹/₄ miles*

A walk through undulating farmland and bridleways with wide sea views along the North Wales coast and across the Dee Estuary to Wirral and Cheshire. The route links the attractive villages of Gwaenysgor and Llanasa.

Start: Begin the walk from the car park and viewpoint about ¹/₂ mile along the lane leading from Gwaenysgor to Prestatyn. *Grid ref: 074 819 (Landranger 116, Explorer 265).*

The walk

1. From the car park walk north along the lane which descends steeply into Prestatyn. At the first sharp left-hand bend turn right onto a signed footpath which runs along the edge of woods to a stile into fields (Clwydian Way). Cross the stile and go ahead for about 30 yards to cross a second stile on the left. Walk along the left edge of the field with widening views seawards and back along the coast to the Great Orme. Before you reach the corner of the field swing right up to a stile on the skyline. Cross the stile and head half-left to the next stile visible ahead, then continue in the same direction across the following field (a little to the right of centre) to another stile.

In the following field bear half-left again through the centre to cross a farm track by two stiles (aim just to the right of conifers). Head half-left again to walk beside woods on the left following power lines overhead. At the end of the woods continue through the following field still beneath the power lines.

31

Field path near Llanasa

In clear conditions there are good views ahead across the Dee Estuary to north Wirral and Liverpool, and down to Talacre Lighthouse near the Point of Ayr.

In the far corner of the field cross the stile and turn right (ignore the stile ahead into fields) along a good broad footpath which is soon enclosed between hedges. This is an old green lane which leads gently down between fields for almost a mile passing a farm on the left to a junction of farm tracks.

2. Turn right along the rough lane and follow this to a T junction on the edge of the picturesque village of Llanasa. Turn right into the village.

Llanasa is one of the most picturesque villages in the area. Sheltered in the folds of a green rolling Devonshire-like landscape, its mellow sandstone cottages could have come straight from a Cotswold village. The hamlet is centred round the eighteenth century church of Saint Asaph and the Red Lion Inn, an excellent local pub offering good ales, bar food and evening meals.

Turn right past the Red Lion Inn and walk along the lane for about ⅓ mile to a stile on the right which leads into fields.

Cross the stile and head diagonally left up the sloping field to a stile in a crossing fence, then continue the diagonal line to a stile in the upper fence on the right. Keep the same diagonal course to reach a stile in the far top corner the next field with a belt of young conifers beyond (Clwydian Way again). Cross two stiles beside the trees and go ahead to a third stile in about 25 yards. Bear diagonally left through the centre of a larger field now to a stile midway along the far hedge/fence. Head diagonally left again aiming to the right of a wood of mature trees.

Don't go through the gate adjacent to the trees, instead bear right along the edge of the field to a stile on the left immediately before a reedy pond. Cross the stile and a second stile a few yards ahead and turn right along the fence to a stile in the corner. Don't cross this stile, instead turn left through the centre of the field following the power lines seen earlier in the walk. In the following fields keep beside woods on the right to enter the farm track again. Turn left along the track.

The track descends with views ahead to Gwaenysgor and Moel Hiraddug. In about ½ mile look for a signed bridleway on the right. Turn right here and follow the right of way between high hedges to a lane.

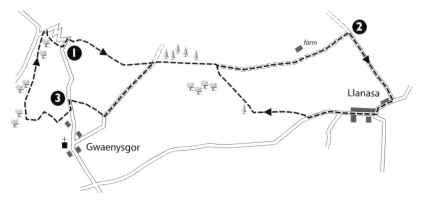

3. If you have had enough you can return to the parking area by turning right along the lane here.

Alternatively, for an additional loop including a short scenic section of the Offa's Dyke Path, turn left along the lane for 150 yards or so and take the signed footpath on the right. Walk through two small fields to join an enclosed path by the old village well. Turn right and follow the path overhung by hedges to emerge in open sloping fields dotted with gorse bushes. Keep left along the lower edge of the field to a stile on the edge of the hillside overlooking Prestatyn and Meliden.

This is a superb viewpoint and in clear weather takes in much of the North Wales coast from Prestatyn past Rhyl and Colwyn Bay to the Great Orme. The green lowland to the left is the Vale of Clwyd which separates the Clwydian Range from the Denbigh Moors. This is backed by the high flat moors of Hiraethog and the mountains of Snowdonia.

Cross the stile and turn right along Offa's Dyke Path which traverses the hillside.

You are less than two miles from the end of Offa's Dyke path for those who have walked it south to north and less than two miles from the start for those making a north south walk. Look out for either very tired or very fresh looking walkers!

Follow the path as it gradually descends the hillside passing above fenced quarries on the left to a lane. Turn right up the lane and in 120 yards or so (immediately after small layby on the right) and about 100 yards before the first sharp right-hand bend, turn right onto a formal edged footpath (not waymarked at the time of writing) into what appears to be overgrown gardens. Shortly there are steps—a few yards after this take the left fork. At the next junction take the stepped path ahead and rise to an access track. Cross this and walk up the grass opposite veering right slightly to the gateway to 'Tyn yr Allt', a large house on the right. Walk ahead past the gate to follow the path directly up through the trees to a lane. Turn right up the lane to return to the parking area.

Cwm & Moel Hiraddug

Distance: *4 miles*

A short but strenuous walk centred on the hamlet of Cwm using woodland and farmland paths with stunning views from Moel Hiraddug.

Start: Begin at the village of Cwm, 1 mile south of Dyserth. Park near 'The Blue Lion'.
Grid ref: 066 774 (Landranger 116, Explorer 265).

The walk

1. Walk up the lane past 'The Blue Lion' and the church, and after about 300 yards, take the signed footpath on the right into fields opposite a cottage. Keep to the field edge in the first field then, after crossing the stream and stile, rise diagonally-right through the following field to a quiet lane.

Turn left along the lane and in about 400 yards, look for a signed footpath on the right. Turn sharp right onto this path and rise through woods with occasional views down to Cwm and access to the shapely Moel Hiraddug.

At a narrow (not very obvious) crossing path (about 250 yards) look for a waymark which directs you left onto a more gentle woodland path soon with a field on the left. After another climb through the trees go over a stile into fields and walk along the edge of the woods on the right with views over to Gwaenysgor and Gop Hill on the left.

Cross a stile by a building down to the left and go ahead to join the access track in about 30 yards. Follow the track ahead to a stile on the left by a gate across the track. Cross the stile and continue ahead beside woods to a stile in the fence on the right. Don't cross this stile, instead follow the path ahead as it curves left down to the lane.

Turn left along the lane and after about 45 yards turn right into fields where a stile and sign indicating Offa's Dyke Path, mark the continuation of the right of way. The path runs beside the right-hand hedge almost to the bottom corner of the field before bearing left slightly to cross a narrow lane by two stiles. In the next field bear half-left along the field edge to two stiles across a farm access track. Rise beside gardens and a cottage on an enclosed footpath to a lane at the hamlet of Marian Cwm.

2. Almost opposite and a little to the left, the path continues over Marian Ffrith, a rounded sheep-grazed hill with a fine panorama from the top. After the stile by a gate bear half-left up the gentle slopes then swing half-right and look for waymarks which indicate the right of way.

Follow the right of way over the hilltop bearing left in the direction of the quarry on Moel Hiraddug to a stone stile in the left-hand corner of the field. Walk down a small field to a stile by a gate. Cross the stile and turn left along a farm track.

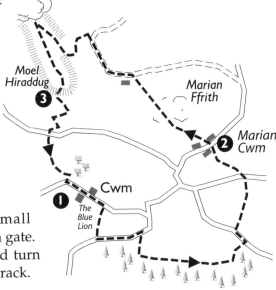

Moel Hiraddug from the woods above Cwm

Pass the farm and continue along the track ignoring signed paths on either side. Where the track turns right, go through the gate straight ahead into a field. Turn left up the field as signed, pass through a gap in a ruined stone wall and continue across the second field to a stone stile in the far wall.

This leads onto open access land which includes the Moel Hiraddug ridge as far north as the quarry overlooking Dyserth.

Walk ahead after the stile and at the end of the wall on the left (about 30 yards) turn left onto a crossing path. This soon begins to curve right before rising more steeply between gorse bushes. Higher up head diagonally right to gain the summit ridge.

In clear weather the view from this hilltop is extensive and takes in much of the Vale of Clwyd, with the dark serrated skyline of Snowdonia in the distance. The coastal resorts from Rhyl to Colwyn Bay can be seen to the northwest, while below on the east bank of Afon Clwyd stands the town of Rhuddlan.

Today, this rather ordinary town gives little impression of its importance during the Middle Ages when it played a key role as a frontier town in the Welsh wars. It developed around the castle built by Edward I in 1277 at the head of what was then a large tidal estuary. This site enabled the castle to be supplied by shipping during a siege, a feature Edward incorporated into all his Welsh castles.

The present ruinous state of Rhuddlan Castle is the result of demolition at the hands of Parliamentarians during the Civil War.

Inland to the northeast you will see the curious cone of Gop Hill crowned by the largest prehistoric cairn in Wales. The cairn is over 60 feet high and formed entirely of drystone mounding. On the southern slopes of the hill are to be found the most northerly signs of Offa's Dyke, leading to the conclusion that it was never finished following Offa's death. Its proposed line is thought to have ended at either Prestatyn or Rhuddlan

3. Turn left along the summit ridge to the highest point at the southern end directly above an aerial and small building. To descend aim to the left of the aerial and building to pick up a path which heads diagonally-right. At the bottom of the steep slope turn left and follow a grass path to a gate below overhead cables. Don't go through the gate, instead, turn right and follow a good path down through gorse and bracken. Where this forks keep left and follow the path as it swings right lower down below gorse to a kissing gate and steps into a lane.

Cross the stile opposite and a little to the left and follow the right of way up the field. Cross a stile at the top of the rise and walk down a sloping field towards woods. Aim for the stile which soon comes into view at the right-hand end of the woods (houses lower down to the right). Cross the stile and follow the path diagonally down through the trees to emerge in a small field with the church ahead. Turn right to a stile in the corner which leads into the lane to complete the walk.

Tremeirchion

Distance: 4³/₄ miles

Easy, hilly walking through farmland, quiet lanes and bridleways in a less frequented section of the Clwydian Range.

Start: Begin the walk in the village of Tremeirchion, 1¹/₂ miles south of Rhuallt on the B5429. Park in the village and start at the 'Salusbury Arms'.

Grid ref: 083 730 (Landranger 116, Explorer 265).

Tremeirchion sits in a grand position on the sunny western slopes of the Clwydian Range just high enough to enjoy wide views across the Vale of Clwyd. Its handful of cottages and farmhouses are gathered around the old church and village pub, named after the local Salusbury family. The church has some fine stained glass portraits of James I, Charles I and Archbishop John Williams—famous for changing sides in the Civil War at Conwy—who had family ties with the Salusburys.

Mrs Thrale, the close friend of the eighteenth century traveller Dr Johnson, also came from this family and settled here with here Italian husband in the Italianate villa known as 'Brynbella' which occupies a lovely position in wooded parkland on the south side of the village.

The walk

1. Walk up the lane past the 'Salusbury Arms' on the left and look for a footpath on the right about 30 yards beyond a farm. Bear half-left across the field to enter a green lane by a large house. Turn right, then left over a stile in a few yards, signposted 'Craig, Tremeirchion'. Descend the field with a house to your left and after a stile, drop into a small bracken covered valley following

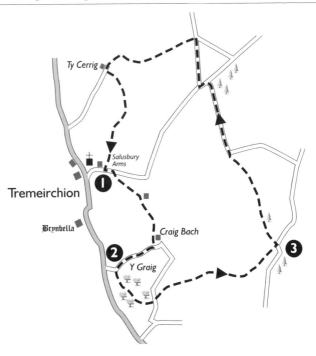

the path beside the stream. Cross two footbridges on the left and bear right up the bank following the waymarks to enter a lane by a cottage on the left ('Craig Bach'). Turn right and walk down the lane for about 500 yards.

2. At a sharp right-hand bend, turn left over a stile, signposted 'Y Graig, Bodfari'. Enter the woods of 'Y Graig Nature Reserve', an area of woodland and limestone outcrops and bear left up to the information board.

Y Graig Nature Reserve was purchased by North Wales Naturalists Trust in 1987 and is noted for its ancient limestone grassland. The shallow dry soils are rich in plant species and the grassland is grazed to prevent the spread of scrub.

Ignoring signs to 'The Summit' and 'Quarry' on either side, continue straight ahead up through the woods. As you break out of the trees (picnic tables and benches up to the left) fine views open out.

The green sweep of the Vale of Clwyd dominates the view; a landscape of farmland and villages reaching north to the coast at Rhyl. Although a picture of peace and tranquillity today, this has not always been the case. It was here that Prince Llywelyn and his brother Dafydd began their final revolt against Edward I in the thirteenth century.

Edward had given lands at nearby Denbigh to Dafydd, but he resented the interference of Edward's officials and called to Llywelyn for his support in a rebellion. Llywelyn answered the call and the two brothers enjoyed initial success, but disaster struck when Llywelyn was killed in a minor skirmish near Builth Wells. Dafydd continued the struggle but he was eventually handed over to Edward and suffered a brutal execution as a traitor at Shrewsbury in 1282.

Dafydd's lands at Denbigh were given to Henry de Lacy, Earl of Lincoln and it was at this time that Denbigh castle and town walls were built in order to hold the area in subjection to the English crown.

Looking back to the slopes of Moel Maenefa near the end of the walk

Work on the defences was halted in 1294 when Welsh rebels captured the town, but the rising was short lived and de Lacy was able to continue the work which was still unfinished when he died in 1311.

Despite the strong defences, the town suffered destruction twice during the fifteenth century. First, during the uprising of Owain Glyndŵr in 1402 and again by Jasper Tudor, Earl of Pembroke in 1468, while the castle was in the hands of the Yorkists during the Wars of the Roses.

During the Civil War the castle was held by Royalists and Charles I stayed there for a few days in 1645. A year later it was surrendered to Parliamentarians who carried out the usual destruction reducing it to the ruins which we see today. The castle and walls are now open to the public.

As the path bears left up the hill turn right over a stile and walk along a narrow footpath to join an access track. Go right along the track to a lane. Turn left here and shortly bear right following the lane up to a house ('Pen y Graig Bach'). Beyond the house the lane continues as an unsurfaced green lane for almost ½ mile.

Looking back from the upper part of the green lane there is a wide view of the northern end of the Vale of Clwyd. Prominent is the tiny cathedral of St Asaph siting boldly in the position which, for almost 1,000 years, earned it the reputation for being the most frequently destroyed religious building in Wales.

This exposed location on the North Wales coast left St Asaph mercilessly open to attacks from across the Irish Sea throughout the Dark Ages. Speaking about this period Michael Senior, in his book, 'Portrait of North Wales' says: "It seems every time anyone invaded North Wales they paused to burn down St Asaph cathedral". As a result, when Edward I tried to move the diocese to Rhuddlan where he had recently built his new castle, he was heavily supported by the bishop and his cannons.

St Asaph did not just suffer destruction at the hands of those who came across the sea though. In the early fifteenth century Owain Glyndŵr, hailed by his countrymen as the new 'Prince of Wales', also put the cathedral to the torch, along with much of nearby Ruthin and Denbigh.

3. At the top of the rise go ahead through a gate into the lane and turn left immediately onto Offa's Dyke Path (sign). Walk beside woods on the right at first, then along field edges and, in the second field bear diagonally-right to a stile in the far fence. Continue ahead (approximately between the two pylons ahead) through the following field to the corner of a quiet lane.

Follow the lane straight ahead to a T junction and turn left. After a few yards turn right into a second lane and at the top of the rise (almost opposite a lane on the right) turn left onto a bridleway, signposted 'Offa's Dyke'. Follow the bridleway which is overhung by trees at first, then, ignoring the Offa's Dyke Path which turns right over a stile, continue ahead descending gently with wide views across the Vale of Clwyd.

Cross a stile by a gate and continue to descend. At the bottom of the slope ignore a path which forks right, instead, go over the stile by a gate and follow a footpath between fields to meet a tarmac lane. Follow the lane ahead and opposite a stone house on the right ('Ty Cerrig'), turn left onto the signed footpath. Keep left passing in front of a stone bungalow to cross a stream before bearing half-right up the following field. Further on keep left along the field edge to a stile in the corner. Stay beside the fence dropping to a stile in the corner of the field again. Bear half-right in the next field and follow a line of stiles ahead through the remaining fields to emerge in the lane beside the 'Salusbury Arms' to complete the walk.

Moel-y-Parc from Bodfari

Distance: *3¹/₂ or 7¹/₄ miles*

An exploration of both sides of the Wheeler valley from the pretty village of Bodfari with grand views throughout. A fairly strenuous route involving serval climbs for the longest and toughest option.

Start: Begin the walk in the village of Bodfari, situated on the B5429 near its junction with the A541 Mold to Denbigh road. The road is wide enough for a few cars to be parked on the northern edge of the village towards Tremeirchion.

Grid ref: 092 702 (Landranger 116, Explorer 265).

Bodfari is a pretty little village gathered around the church and seventeenth century Dinorben Arms. It is situated just high enough to enjoy wide views across the Vale of Clwyd and the Wheeler valley. A Roman road is thought by some to have passed through this gap in the hills and there is reputed to have been a camp nearby, but there seems to be little agreement. The village has two ancient wells, one of which can be seen inside the 'Dinorben Arms'.

The walk

1. Walk back towards the church and the 'Dinorben Arms' and immediately before the first houses on the left (opposite 'The Old Rectory') turn left through a gate and walk towards the church. Just before the gate turn left over a stile by the cemetery wall and walk up the field edge towards woods. At the edge of the trees turn right over an iron stile and follow a faint path straight ahead along the edge of the wood. The path disappears here and there but takes a contouring line at first before rising leftwards just before a quarry to bring you to a fence leading into sloping fields. If you are in the right place you should be in a field corner with a fence/hedge to your right and a sloping field ahead with more woods on the skyline.

There is no stile at the time of writing so you must climb the fence. Walk directly up the field trending left and passing a line of trees which mark an old field boundary. The stile in the top corner of the field is hidden amongst gorse but is not overgrown. Cross the stile and keep left along the field edge to a stile to the right of the corner.

You are now on the Offa's Dyke Path. Look right for a superb view over the Vale of Clwyd with the Clwydian Range to the left and the distant Hiraethog moors on the right. The medieval hill town of Denbigh can be seen in the valley with the Llantysilio ridge at the head of the vale on the skyline.

Climb the stile and take the footpath ahead. As you approach farm

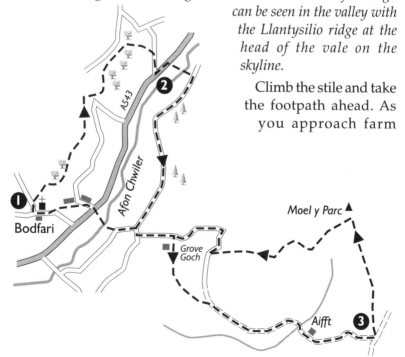

buildings bear left up the bank to a stile by a small crag. Continue ahead above the farm before dropping to a stile which leads onto the access track. Turn left and follow the track down to a gate.

Go through the gate following the track as it swings sharp right and turn sharp left almost immediately onto a good footpath (Offa's Dyke Path continues down the track). Follow this path through woods with fields to the left until you reach a driveway. Turn left along the drive for about 25 yards then turn right between outbuildings and farm machinery onto a descending footpath. Take the first right turn in 150 yards or so and where this forks shortly (about 25 yards), keep left. At a narrow lane turn right and walk down to the main road.

Bodfari from the flanks of Moel-y-Parc

2. Unfortunately there is an unavoidable section along the busy main road here but it is soon over (take care). Turn left along the road and in about 150 yards take the signed footpath on the right. Follow the path ahead to cross the river (Afon Wheeler) by a footbridge and go ahead again to the lane.

Turn right along the lane for about ³/₄ mile. (At the time of writing there is a severely obstructed public right of way through the fields on the left about half way along the lane. If this has been opened up it will eliminate half of the section along the lane to emerge opposite the driveway to 'Grove Goch')

Pass a lane on the right signed for the ODP and take the next left also carrying the ODP sign. Walk up the narrow lane and at the end of a high red brick wall on the right, turn right down the driveway to 'Grove Goch'. Almost immediately bear left to a stile. Cross the stile and walk through two small fields with a large house over to the right. After the third stile bear half-left up through three fields to a stile in the top corner of the last field which leads onto the open gorse covered hillside.

Go ahead beside the fence and where the path forks shortly, keep left rising to a T junction with a broader path. Turn right and follow this path which contours the open gorse and bracken covered hillside.

Curve round with the path (ODP) into a sheltered valley with farms and cottages down to the right, to eventually reach a T junction with an unsurfaced gravel track. Turn right along the track which descends a little way then begins a long rise to the bwlch between Moel Y Parc and Penycloddiau. This is easily followed and waymarked for the Offa's Dyke Path.

3. At the top of the pass don't go through the gate across the track, instead turn left on the signed footpath to 'Moel y Parc' which runs beside the right-hand fence.

Continue until the fence on the right turns right and there is a small cairn immediately ahead.

The view is extensive from here and takes in both the Vale of Clwyd, Denbigh Moors and Snowdonia to the west as well as east across Flintshire, Wirral, Cheshire and the Lancashire coast to the Pennines.

From the corner of the fence take the signed path left ('Aifft') which drops steeply down to a small bwlch where a squat waymarker indicates a crossing path. Turn right here on the path signed 'Afonwen'. As you descend the path curves left (ignore a right fork) to eventually run beside small fields down to the right. Continue to a large gate which leads into woods. Follow the obvious path through the trees to a junction. Turn sharp right here and follow another good footpath to a tarmac lane near cottages. Turn left down the steeply descending lane.

Pass the driveway to 'Grove Goch' and at the T junction turn right then left again. Look for the signed Offa's Dyke Path a little way down the lane on the right, which cuts directly through fields to a footbridge over the river to reach the A541. Cross the road to the village store opposite and turn left along the village road rather than the A541. Where the road bends right, bear left onto the signed footpath which brings you back into Bodfari. Turn right past the Dinorben Arms and the church to complete the walk.

Caerwys &
Ysceifiog Lake

Distance: 6½ miles

Good field and woodland paths are used to explore a surprisingly varied area between the ancient villages of Caerwys and Ysceifiog.

Start: There is limited parking available in a small layby just off the A541 near Afonwen Craft Centre.
Grid ref: 131 715 (Landranger 116, Explorer 265).

Caerwys is a quiet out-of-the-way village today, but in the past was one of the three most important towns in Flintshire, being one of the few places where cases could be judged according to Welsh law. Evidence for this can be seen in its grid-like layout and large square. It was founded as a Borough in 1290 but seems to have never flourished, probably as a result of its unusual location and poor communications. It is now the smallest town in Wales.

The walk

1. Return to the main road and turn left. Walk along the road to the 'Pwll Gwyn Hotel' and immediately before the car park turn right onto a signed right of way which begins as a short access road. At a fork in a few yards keep left. As the path steepens there is a strip of woodland on the right.

This is Pwll-gwyn Wood and is managed by the Woodland Trust. A circular permissive path on the right can be followed through the wood. Higher up an information board gives some local information on the wood and explains some of the plants which can be found here due to the unusual geology.

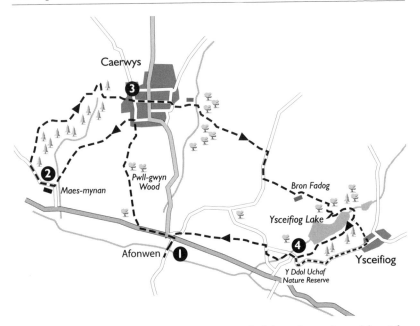

After the wood cross a stile into a field and go ahead beside the right-hand hedge. Enter a track and turn right. At the road on the outskirts of Caerwys turn left ('Pen-y-Cefn Road') and almost immediately, at a sharp right-hand bend turn left down an access road. Where this swings right into the golf course (also a signed footpath), continue straight ahead on a good footpath which descends gradually with woods on the right in the lower half. Don't be tempted by any of the paths which lead off right into the woods. Lower down cross a stile into a small field and go ahead to join a lane by the entrance to a sand quarry.

2. Turn right up the lane ignoring a signed footpath on the left immediately after 'Maes-mynan' farm buildings. Higher up the lane turn right onto a waymarked footpath into the woods of Coed Maes-mynan. The path rises through the trees to run beside fields on the left higher up.

At the top of the rise and at a point where the path begins to descend, turn left over a stile by a gate in the fence and keep right along the field edge by woods passing a small limestone quarry and the remains of a lime kiln. After the quarry a stile leads into a large field and the right of way continues beside the fence. Just before the next field corner turn right over a stile in the fence and drop into Coed Maes-mynan again.

At a T junction turn left for about 40 yards before bearing right onto a footpath again. Follow this path down into the bottom of the valley with a small sewage works on the right. Rise beside the enclosing fence to join a crossing path. Follow this right for about 15 yards and look for a narrow footpath which soon bears left up through the trees. Follow this and at the top of the bank cross a stile and walk across a narrow golf course fairway, then along a path straight ahead bordered by young conifers on the right. Keep to the right of the club house to a stile into an enclosed footpath. Follow this to the road.

3. Turn left then immediately right into 'Drovers Lane' passing 'Pinfold Caerwys', a walled enclosure on the left where stray animals were contained in earlier years. At the next junction turn right and walk along the road into the square and turn left.

Pass 'The Royal Oak' and continue until the road turns right. Continue straight ahead here down the hill to the trout farm. Walk past the front of the house to a stile and take the signed path ('Ysceifiog') to the right. Follow this path to a stile at the edge of the woods. Go over the stile and turn left up the field to a stile by a large gate in the upper fence. Climb the bank after the stile and walk directly across the following large field. Keep to the left of a small area of trees and scrub at the far side of the field and look for a stile hidden in the corner to the left. Bear right in the next field and head for the stile about 20 yards left of the field corner. Walk ahead through a narrow field to enter the lane by a stile beside the drive to 'Marian Cocaldiad Barn'.

Turn right along the lane and in about 250 yards turn left onto a signed footpath which passes through an area of scrub then heads off across the field. Bear half-right in this field (Ysceifiog church tower straight ahead) towards the roof of a large farmhouse.

Ysceifiog Lake

The faint circular mound in the middle of the field is thought to be an ancient earthwork, possibly a defended farmstead.

Cross a second field to join a farm track immediately before 'Bron Fadog' farm. Turn left along the track and follow this between outbuildings. Keep ahead and after the last small shed on the right bear right to a gateway (farmhouse ahead). Go through the gateway, turn sharp left through a second gateway and walk along the top of a sloping field with woods below and occasional glimpses of Ysceifiog Lake through the trees. Cross a well hidden stile in the left-hand corner of the field and head through the centre of the following field aiming to the right of a farmhouse. A stile leads into woods and in a few yards there is a T junction and a fingerpost. Turn right ('Ysceifiog') and follow the path down through the trees to the shores of the lake.

At a T junction turn right and cross the stream by a footbridge turning right to follow a path running parallel to the lake shore a few yards away through the trees.

(Alternatively, you can extend the walk slightly to take in the pretty village of Ysceifiog and its cosy little pub by heading directly up the sloping field after crossing the footbridge, instead of turning right along the lake. At the top of the rise an enclosed footpath leads between gardens into the village. Turn left for the pub and the village centre, right along the lane to continue the walk. This leads down to 'Y Ddol Uchaf Nature Reserve'.)

This picturesque lake was created by the Earl of Denbigh in 1904 as a private fishing lake, an activity which is still enjoyed here. Despite the artificial nature of the pool it certainly enhances this already lovely spot framed by the steep wooded sides of the Nant-gwyn valley. The path which can be seen running along the water's edge, along with the board walk at the inflow, is for the use of fishermen not the public. Coots, moorhens, swans and ducks will often be seen here.

4. Cross a stile (at the end of the path), turn right and continue to a narrow lane. Turn right along the lane and keep right at a fork in a few yards. Very shortly bear left into 'Y Ddol Uchaf Nature Reserve'.

There is an information board here giving details of the unique flora and fauna to be found in this calcium-rich environment. The nature reserve has been designated a Site of Special Scientific Importance (SSSI).

Follow the footpath past the information board and at a fork in about 120 yards bear right. Pass pools on the right and cross a small footbridge. Stay on the main path and near the edge of the reserve turn right over a stile by a gate into the lane. Turn right up the lane and at a turning on the right, go left onto an access track. Pass outbuildings and keep ahead to pass a sand quarry on the left.

At the end of the path cross a stile into fields. Keep ahead through the fields to a lane and turn left. In a few yards turn left again and at the main road cross over to complete the walk.

Penycloddiau & Moel Arthur

Distance: *4¹/₄ or 6¹/₂ miles*

A long and fairly strenuous route along the Clwydian ridge visiting two Iron Age hillforts with steep climbs and descents between. Paths are good throughout and views are extensive in clear conditions.

Start: Begin the walk at Llangwyfan Forest car park situated at the highest point of the lane which runs between Llangwyfan and Nannerch.
Grid ref: 139 668 (Landranger 116, Explorer 265).

The walk

1. From the little car park follow the signed Offa's Dyke Path northwards into the plantations. Immediately you are presented with three forestry tracks; take the right-hand track for a few yards before bearing right onto a much narrower, though well used footpath which runs along the very edge of the trees.

Just before the earthworks which encircle the hilltop of Penycloddiau, turn right over a stile and follow the signed footpath to the summit cairn at the northern end of the enclosure.

The earthworks which encircle the summit form the largest Iron Age enclosure on the Clwydian Range. Over 50 acres lie within its triple banks which are still remarkably well preserved. The earthworks are such a prominent feature of the hilltop that they have given it its name—Penycloddiau means 'head of the trenches'.

Thankfully the nearby conifer plantations of the Llangwyfan Forest have stopped short of the summit enclosure enabling the walker to enjoy extensive views over the Vale of Clwyd in fine weather. The distant peaks of Snowdonia are visible in clear conditions.

2. From the summit follow the Offa's Dyke Path northwards out of the enclosure and across the open moors for almost 1 mile to a pass crossed by unsurfaced green lanes.

Turn sharp left here onto a bridleway which contours the hillside for about 2¼ miles.

If your walk along the exposed ridge was windy you will be better able to enjoy the views westwards to the Vale of Clwyd from the relative shelter of this lower path.

As you leave the open deciduous woods at Nant Simon where the path loops left to cross a stream, look for a path which bears left into conifers just before a gate. If you want to shorten the walk, follow this path back to the car

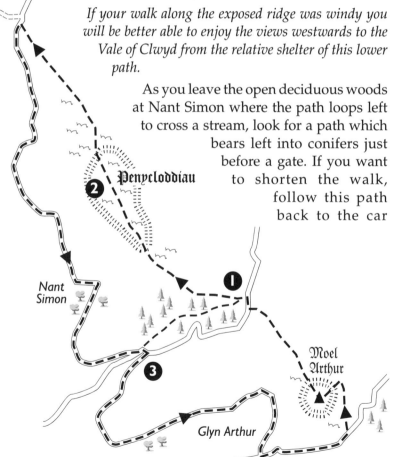

On the bwlch at the northern end of Penycloddiau

park at point **1.** For a longer round, continue through the gate ahead and follow the track to a road.

3. Turn left along the road and where it turns left (about 150 yards), turn right onto a bridleway again. After a gate near a house, the right of way continues as a narrower path which contours the hillside for about 1¾ miles to join the hill road above Glyn Arthur.

Turn left along the road and walk up to the little car park at the top of the pass where you rejoin the Offa's Dyke Path.

Follow the signed Offa's Dyke Path on the left. This takes a rightward diagonal line aiming for a broad shoulder to the right of the summit of Moel Arthur. At the top of the rise a path on the left leads through heather to the exposed summit.

Like Penycloddiau, this hilltop is crowned by the earthworks of an Iron Age hill fort built over 2,000 years ago by the Celts who inhabited this part of Wales in the years before the Roman invasion.

At almost 1,500 feet the view is extensive and you are treated to a bird's eye view of the Vale of Clwyd. Eastwards, you will be able to pick out the long arm of the Wirral peninsula with the hills between Beeston and Frodsham rising from the Cheshire Plain. To the south, the summit cone of Moel Famau, highest point on the Clwydian Range, rises above the surrounding moors, while the distant peaks of the Arans fill the skyline to the southwest.

From here continue northwards to rejoin the main Offa's Dyke Path near a stile which leads into grazing fields. Follow the obvious path down the sloping fields to the road. Turn right here and the forest car park lies a few yards away.

Bryn Golau from Nannerch

Distance: *6 miles*

An exploration of a little-known area to the east of the main Clwydian ridge centred on the attractive village of Nannerch. In clear conditions there are wide views into and across the Wheeler valley. A combination of bridleways and field paths.

Start: Begin in the village of Nannerch which lies just off the A541 about 5 miles west of Mold.

Grid ref: 167 694 (Landranger 116, Explorer 265).

Nannerch is a small village gathered tightly around the church and village pub. The church is quite recent dating from the 1850s and is the work of T.H. Wyatt. Its notable features are a broach spire, an east window by Gibbs and a remarkable brass chandelier. It also has a grand marble monument and sarcophagus to a prominent member of the Mostyn family.

The walk

1. With the 'Cross Foxes' on your right, walk north out of the village past the church and take the first lane on the left. Pass cottages on the left and take the signed ('Cilffordd') bridleway on the right. The path drops between hedges for about 500 yards to a gate with a cottage beyond. Bear left on a path which, in 150 yards, continues the descent to a lane. Turn left and walk along the lane to a T junction.

The earth mound to the left known as 'Bryn Rug' appears to be the earthworks of a motte and bailey castle of the Norman period.

Cross the road and follow the footpath almost opposite which runs beside the stream. Continue close to the stream weaving in and out of trees to eventually enter fields by a stile. Keep ahead with the fence on the left until you are level with a house visible up to your right. Turn right up the field at this point to a stile into the lane opposite the house ('Graybrun Kennels'). To shorten the walk turn left down the lane and continue from point 3.

For the full walk turn right up the rising lane. Where this levels there are views to the right across the valley to Ysceifiog Church.

At a T junction turn left up the hill. Ignore the first lane on the right, continuing up the lane ahead. Take the next turning on the right—a short access track leading to a field gate on the left and the gate to 'Penymynydd and Rose Cottage' ahead. Go through the gate ahead and follow the access track to the first house ('Rose Cottage'). Immediately after the house bear left at a fork, then left again before the next gate onto a signed footpath. Follow the enclosed footpath and immediately before a small gate into a cottage garden ('Pen-y-Mynydd'), cross a stile in the fence on the left. Turn right by the fence to pass above the cottage. At the

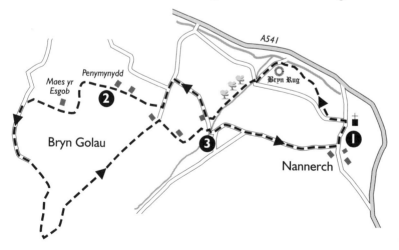

Looking up to the main Clwydian ridge from Bryn Golau

end of the fence adjacent to the cottage, don't follow the path which bears half-right down beside the fence, instead, bear half-left and rise a little to pick up a faint contouring sheep path.

These open fields give wide views across the valley to Caerwys, Ysceifiog church and Halkyn Mountain.

2. Head for a mast on the distant hillside and continue until you can look down into a valley with a stone farm ('Maes yr Esgob') below. Bear left to contour the slope and descend slightly to a large field gate in the corner. Go through the gate and follow the path ahead by the fence/hedge with the farm down to your right. Continue ahead until you reach the farm access track just beyond the farm. Turn left and walk down the track passing another house on the left.

Lower down continue ahead where a lane joins from the right by a cattle grid. At a distinct fork further on, bear left onto a much rougher track. This track rises gradually for about ¹/₂ mile.

Eventually you pass an access track on the left which leads to a cottage. Ignore this, continuing ahead for 200 yards or so where a well hidden stile on the left leads into a field (immediately before the track forks). Cross the stile and bear half-left directly across the field to a stile and large field gate. Go over the stile and keep ahead beside the left-hand fence. In the next field the fence on the left is replaced by a bank topped by bent hawthorn bushes. At the end of these cross a stile by a gateway and walk directly ahead through the following field.

After the next stile continue ahead, soon between a fence and an intermittent hedge and trees. A final stile takes you through a small area of scrub and trees to join a track by a house on the left. In a few yards turn right, not down the obvious farm track, but a hidden path immediately after the track which runs parallel to it on the opposite side of the hedge. The path is enclosed at first with a large tank to the left, then keeps along the right-hand field edge to a stile in the corner. Keep ahead again through the next field to a second stile a few yards to the left of the corner. Turn left along the hedge to the far corner, then turn sharp right down with the fence to pass to the right of a cottage.

Go through a gate adjacent to the cottage and go ahead down the access track. Immediately after the cottage garden turn left (by telegraph pole) through a field gate and keep along the left-hand field edge to a stile in the top left corner. Cross this, then bear half-right through the field to a gate in the far fence. This leads into a small garden used as a pet's cemetery. Walk forward a few yards then turn left through a gap in the conifer hedge and make your way along the lower edge of the garden to reach the lane by a gate.

3. Turn right down the lane soon passing cottages which were once millers buildings. Continue along the lane back to Nannerch ignoring turnings on the right (almost 1 mile).

Moel Llys-y-coed & Moel Dywyll

Distance: *6 or 8 miles*

A long and quite strenuous route if you take the longest option which uses old drovers' roads to access two minor tops on the main Clwydian ridge (Moel Famau can also be included) and the attractive village of Cilcain. Footpaths are excellent throughout.

Start: Begin at the forest car park on the pass immediately south of Moel Arthur. *Grid ref: 147 658 (Landranger 116, Explorer 265).*

The walk

1. From the car park take the signed Offa's Dyke Path south (left) up the steep northern slopes of Moel Llys-y-coed (a name which may indicate the existence of an early court —*'llys'*).

At the top of the rise look back for a view of Moel Arthur and the folded spurs which tumble west into the Vale of Clwyd. Moel Arthur can be seen to be one of the best defensive sites in the range—a steep conical hill needing minimal fortification.

The walk across the plateau is easy and fairly level with wide views into the Vale of Clwyd and along the ridge ahead to Moel Famau in clear conditions.

At a pass with cross paths you can take a shortcut back to 'Cilcain' by taking the signed path on the left. Continue from point 3 walk 11 (page 73). Alternatively, continue ahead over Moel Dywyll.

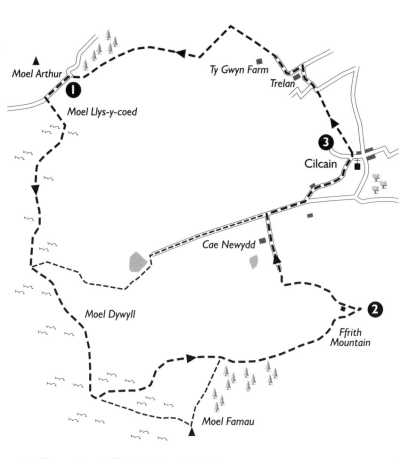

Follow the Offa's Dyke Path between two cairns on Moel Dywyll. After this the path drops before beginning the climb to Moel Famau. At the point where you begin the final steep climb to the summit, take the signed footpath over the stile on the left. (You could of course continue to the summit of Moel Famau for a longer and more strenuous route and descend via the Cilcain path.)

The path contours the slope below Moel Famau to meet the descent path to Cilcain at a corner of conifer plantations. (If you continued to the summit of Moel Famau you will join here from the right and turn right.) Go straight ahead here walking beside conifers on the right at first, then with the open pastures of the rounded Ffrith Mountain on the right. There are good views into the wooded eastern cwms of Moel Famau from this path. Lower down go through a gate and continue to descend until you pass a ruined building on the left.

This is the remains of a Second World War decoy control station designed to attract German bombers away from Merseyside.

2. About 50 yards beyond the ruins turn sharp left onto the access track to a house which can be seen about 250 yards away. Pass the house on the right-hand side and follow a bridleway ahead through several fields eventually with the open bracken covered hillside to the left.

Further on the path swings right using railway sleepers to cross a wet area. After a gate follow a descending green lane passing a stone cottage ('Cae Newydd') and turn right at a T junction. At the tarmac lane turn left and walk along the lane to Cilcain.

Cilcain is an attractive village centred on St Mary's church and the White Horse Inn. See the following route for notes on the village's history.

3. At the end of the lane turn right and take the signed footpath on the left between the village hall and small car park opposite the church. Pass through a small playing field, then take a direct line through the following fields. At the end of the first field the stile is to the right and at the back of a small hollow partly filled with rubbish. Cut directly through the following fields to a lane. Go ahead along the lane and straight ahead again at a sharp left-hand bend in a few yards. After a dip and a rise, turn left at a T junction (beside 'Trelan'). Continue for about 500 yards to the end of the lane and where the drive to 'Ty Gwyn Farm' swings left, keep ahead on the signed bridleway. At a T junction with a broad green lane turn left and make a steady rise.

Gop Hill from the lane to Gwaenysgor (walk 1)

Wind-bent trees on Bryn Golau (walk 8)

Moel Arthur from Bryn Golau (walk 8)

Corn fields near Nannerch (walk 8)

Moel Famau from Moel Dywyll during early September (walk 9)

Moel Famau from the fields below Moel y Gaer (walk 10)

Moel Famau from Loggerheads Country Park (walk 12)

Foel Fenlli from Moel Famau (walk 14)

Moel Famau from Moel Findeg (walks 13 & 16)

Bryn Alyn (walks 16 & 18)

Limestone pavement on Bryn Alyn (walks 16 & 18)

Foel Fenlli from Moel Gyw (walk 17)

*Looking west across the Vale of Clwyd from the lane below Moel Waun
(walk 20)*

Moel Famau seen across the heather moorland of Moel Dywyll

The track eventually meets a contouring track at a T junction and a gate. Go through the gate and turn right along the track heading towards the conifer plantations which fill the valley below Moel Arthur.

Soon Moel Arthur comes into view, its conical outline looking a little out of place among such rounded neighbours. The rocks and geological structure in this area suggest the existence of gold, but to date none has been found.

Follow the track to the lane and narrow pass separating Moel Arthur from the plateau of Moel Llys-y-coed to complete the walk.

Moel Famau from Llangynhafal

Distance: *5½ miles*

A strenuous walk on the steep western slopes of Moel Famau high above the Vale of Clwyd. Superb views into the Vale and across to the mountains of Snowdonia are the reward for such hard work. Footpaths are generally good although a short section on the descent to Moel y Gaer requires careful route finding.

Start: Just to the south of the village of Llangynhafal there is a crossroads and about 200 yards south of this (on the lane to Hirwaen), there is a small layby with room for half a dozen cars or so. *Grid ref: 130 632 (Landranger 116, Explorer 265).*

The walk

1. On the opposite side of the lane and a few yards back towards Llangynhafal, take the signed path across a small field to enter another lane. Turn right and follow the lane up to St Cynhafal's parish church.

Pass the church and continue up the rising lane to a house ('Dol-y-Caeau') on the left (about ⅓ mile). A few yards before the house take the signed footpath on the right which shortly leads onto the open hillside. The path contours above fields on the right with wide views across the Vale of Clwyd.

Continue passing a striking Scot's pine on the right at one point. A little beyond this the path veers left away from the walled fields on the right and down into a small valley. Cross the stream and rise to a fork beside a fingerpost. Turn left here and follow

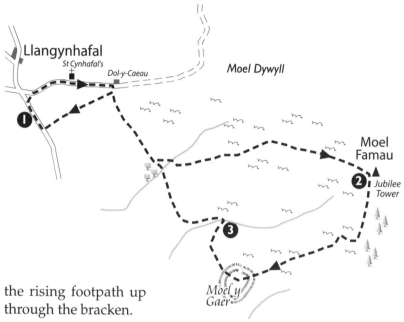

the rising footpath up
through the bracken.

As the angle eases the
Jubilee Tower on the summit of Moel Famau comes into view.
Continue on the obvious path which, as you approach the
summit, curves left to join the Offa's Dyke Path at a T junction
on the broad whale back ridge. Turn right and rise steeply up to
the summit.

*From the summit you can enjoy one of the finest panoramas in
northeast Wales, particularly west across the Vale of Clwyd and the
Denbigh Moors to the peaks of Snowdonia on the far horizon. North
and south the views are along the switchback ridge of the Clwydian
Range, while to the east lies the distant lowland of the Cheshire Plain,
scarred by the Deeside and Merseyside industrial belts.*

*The ruined tower which crowns the highest point was built in 1810
to commemorate the 50th year of the reign of King George III. It was
originally designed in the Egyptian style to reach a height of 150 feet,
but the plans were never fully carried out and the structure that was
built collapsed in 1862 following a series of gales. Attempts to restore*

the tower for Queen Victoria's Golden Jubilee in 1887 were a failure and the modest structure which we now see is all that remains.

2. Take the Offa's Dyke Path south from the summit (signed 'Bwlch Penbarra'). After the initial steep descent the path levels with conifer woods on the left.

The next section down to Moel y Gaer hillfort needs careful route finding. Continue until a small heathery rise on the left obscures the trees briefly and there is a bench on the right (inscribed 'Tower View 1st April 2002 Tony Christopher'). A few yards further on turn right onto a narrow footpath through the heather. This soon swings rightwards, back towards Moel Dywyll with its two summit cairns. At a point where the path becomes completely level (about 150 yards from the bench), look for a very narrow but visible path on the left. This path soon begins to descend and Moel y Gaer hillfort comes into view below.

Continue the descent down through bracken to a broad col to enter the hillfort through a gap in the earthworks. In the centre of the enclosure a small stone cairn marks the highest point.

Like the other hillforts on the Clwydian Range, Moel y Gaer was constructed by Celtic tribes in the centuries before the Roman invasion and is unusual in being the only hillfort not situated on the main ridge itself. It is, however, easy to see why the site was chosen with steep ground on three sides, the only approach is from the east via this narrow connecting ridge which would have been easy to defend.

Head northwest from the summit (towards the western end of the Vale of Clwyd where the hills meet the flat land) crossing the earthworks and descending to a well hidden stile in the fence below. Cross the stile and turn right around a large area of gorse, then diagonally-right down the sloping field to where fences meet the stream in the bottom of the valley. At the bottom of the slope before the fence, turn right passing a waymarker post and continuing ahead to a second post. Turn sharp left here as directed between gorse on the left and the fence to the right to reach a gate. Go through the gate and turn left over the stream to follow

Paths near the summit of Moel Famau

the footpath above a small bracken filled valley down to the left.

3. After a slight rise the path swings right to run beside walled fields on the left. Continue on this path eventually joining the outward route just before the solitary Scot's pine seen earlier.

Just before the path joins the lane bear left down to a gate. Go through the gate and follow a sunken bridleway down to the lane where a right turn will take you back to the layby to complete the walk.

Moel Famau from Cilcain

Distance: *5³/₄ miles*

An ascent of the highest summit in the Clwydian Range from the attractive village of Cilcain. The walking is both steep and strenuous in parts but extensive views from the summit in clear conditions more than compensate.

Start: Begin in the little village of Cilcain, 3 miles north of Loggerheads. Limited parking is available in a small layby on the outskirts of the village. This can be reached from the 'White Horse Inn' by passing the church and taking the first lane on the left. In about 500 yards the lane drops to cross a stream and bends sharp left. Park on the left here.

Grid ref: 172 647 (Landranger 116, Explorer 265).

Cilcain, an attractive old village gathered around the ancient church of St. Mary and the White Horse Inn, is ideally situated for an ascent of Moel Famau ('mother hill'), the highest peak in the Clwydian Range.

In earlier centuries the village lay on the meeting point of several old drovers' roads which crossed the Clwydian ridge as well as a pilgrims' route which linked St. Winnifred's Well at Holywell with St. David's in South Wales and would have been far busier than today, isolated as it now is at the end of a cul-de-sac.

One possible interpretation of the village name may give a clue to its earliest origins—'cil' meaning a nook, corner or retreat and 'cain' meaning fair—thus Cilcain was, and still is, a 'fair retreat'. The possible origin of this 'fair retreat', according to one story, is that St. Eurgain (of Llaneurgain or Northop) withdrew to a cell here in Nant Cain to escape persecution during a period of religious intolerance.

The walk

1. Opposite the parking area, take the straight unsurfaced lane on the right and almost immediately turn left through a gate ('Tyddyn-y-Foel'). After about 20 yards turn right over stone steps into fields and follow the right of way along the left-hand field edge until a stile leads into a green lane near a junction of bridleways.

Turn left here and follow the green lane to a gate and stile. Immediately after this the track forks; take the path ahead which is soon surfaced with large railway sleepers and curves left to contour the hillside. Keep straight ahead through several fields which can be boggy in wet conditions to a gate near a cottage on the right. Pass the cottage and walk ahead down the rough access track towards a gate. Immediately before the gate turn sharp right onto a good signed path which rises onto the rounded slopes of Ffrith Mountain.

Continue on the rising path which becomes less steep higher up

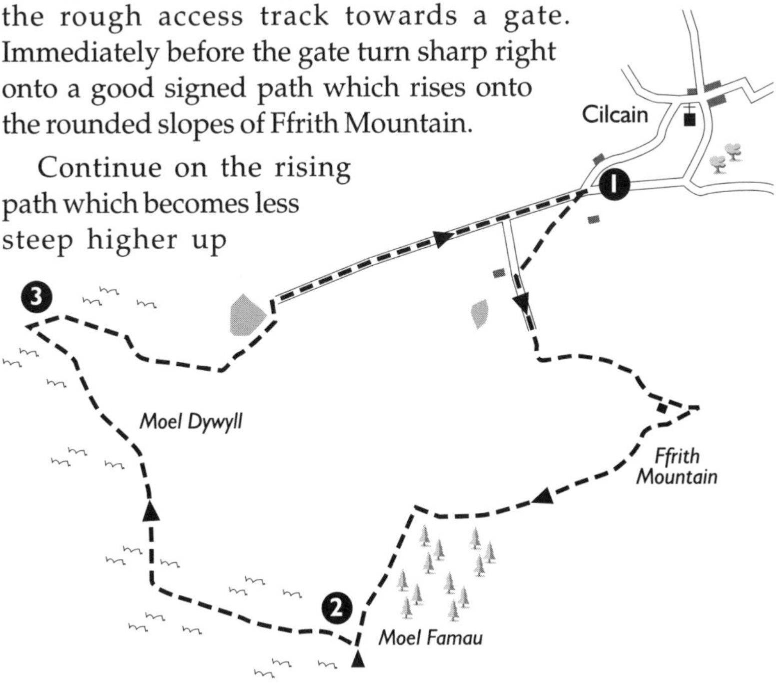

Cilcain

Moel Dywyll

Ffrith Mountain

Moel Famau

Moel Famau from Cilcain

with views left into the long sweeping valleys which cut into Moel Famau's eastern slopes. At a junction of paths turn left up towards the summit with conifer plantations to your left

From the summit there is a wide panorama, particularly west across the Vale of Clwyd and the Denbigh Moors to the peaks of Snowdonia which peep over the horizon. To the north the radio mast at Moel y Parc is visible and obscures the northern end of the Clwydian ridge. Southwards, the rolling tops dissolve into the shapeless moors of Llandegla and the Llantysilio hills. To the east lies the lowland of the Cheshire Plain and the Deeside and Merseyside industrial belts.

The ruined tower which crowns the highest point was built in 1810 to commemorate the 50th year of the reign of King George III. It was originally designed in the Egyptian style to reach a height of 150 feet, but the plans were never fully carried out and the structure that was built collapsed in 1862 following a series of gales. Attempts to restore the tower for Queen Victoria's Golden Jubilee in 1887 were a failure and the modest structure which we now see is all that remains.

2. From the Jubilee Tower follow waymarked Offa's Dyke Path north over Moel Dywyll with its twin cairns. Beyond Moel Dywyll, drop to a little pass where a gated track crosses the hills between Cilcain and Llangynhafal.

3. Turn right through the gate (signposted 'Cilcain 2.5 m') and follow the track for about 200 yards before bearing right onto a signed path which runs between stone walls towards a small reservoir. Keep to the right of the reservoir ignoring all other footpaths and join the access road just below the dam.

Turn right here and follow the unsurfaced lane/track for about 1 mile back to the parking area to complete the walk.

The Alyn Gorge & Moel Famau

Distance: *8³/₄ miles*

An excellent walk along the Alyn Gorge—with its mining legacy and beautiful woods—to the village of Cilcain, with a return over Moel Famau and a traverse of its eastern cwms. Good paths throughout.

Start: Begin the walk at Loggerheads Country Park. There is parking available at the Visitor Centre (pay and display) along with a café, a small outdoor shop and toilets. An alternative start could be made from the village of Cilcain (see the start for the previous route).

Grid ref: 197 625 (Landranger 116, Explorer 265).

The walk

1. From the car park walk past the Visitor Centre, café, toilets and the small outdoor shop to cross the river by the footbridge. Turn left immediately onto the path which runs beside the river. Stay on the main path and don't take any of the alternatives which bear left to run close to the river.

At a gate, take the signed 'Leete Path' straight ahead.

This path follows the line of an old leat which can be seen quite clearly here and there. Built in 1823 by John Taylor of the Mold Mines Company, it was originally 6 feet wide and 4 feet deep and was designed to carry water to power waterwheel-driven mining machinery lower down the valley. It was abandoned in 1845.

Stay on the 'Leete Path' ignoring other paths eventually joining the drive to 'Alyn Boarding Kennels'. Walk down the drive to a narrow lane and take the path opposite through mature beech woods alive with colour in the spring and autumn.

The path is now high above the river and occasional views open out across the valley to Moel Famau, its smooth contours contrasting with the craggy outlines of this eastern side of the River Alyn.

At one point you pass the half buried remains of a small bridge which once spanned the leat. Ignore the right fork here continuing straight ahead by the leat instead.

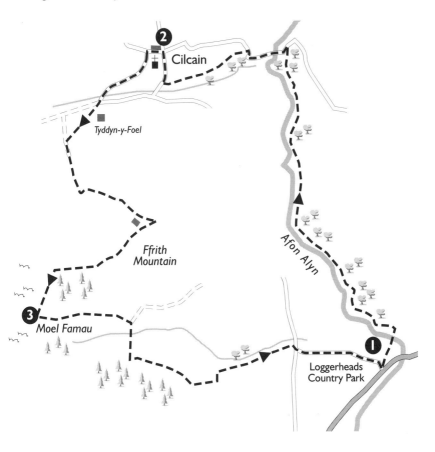

A little further on a footbridge takes you over Devil's Gorge—a legacy of the lead mining carried out all along the valley here. Fortunately operations ceased before too much damage was done to this beautiful valley.

Eventually the path swings right to join the road near the village of Pantymwyn. Turn left, walk down the hill and cross the little bridge, barely wide enough for modern vehicles to use. Ignore the signed bridleway soon after the bridge on the left, instead, stay on the rising lane and take the signed footpath ('Pentre') ahead at the top of the rise where the lane bends sharp right. Follow an enclosed path at first, then enter fields by a stile. Keep left along the field edge and in a field or two enter a field recently planted with young trees.

This is Coed y Felin, named after the nearby medieval water mill and was created by the Woodland Trust as part of the 'Woods on your doorstop' millennium project. At the top of the field on your right you will see a group of carved badgers.

Either turn right up the field past the carved badgers and then bear left along the top hedge to the lane, or continue a little further and turn left between two posts in the fence. Follow the path down a wooded bank to a path junction and turn right (ignore footbridge on the left) passing a small pool to reach the lane. Which ever route you take, turn right along the lane to the village of Cilcain.

2. Turn left at the 'White Horse Inn' and left again immediately after the churchyard. Walk along the descending lane with its grand view of the curving hillside of Moel Famau.

After a short descent the lane bends sharp left. Turn right onto a farm track here, then immediately left through a gate ('Tyddyn-y-Foel'). After about 20 yards cross stone steps into fields on the right. Follow the right of way along field edges until a stile leads into a green lane near a junction of bridleways.

Turn left here and follow the green lane to a gate and stile. Immediately after this the track forks; take the path ahead which

Crossing the footbridge over Devil's Gorge, one of the old lead mines

is soon surfaced with large railway sleepers and curves left to contour the hillside. Keep straight ahead through several fields which can be boggy in wet conditions to a gate near a cottage on the right. Pass the cottage and walk ahead down the rough access track towards a gate. Immediately before the gate turn sharp right onto a good signed path which rises onto the rounded slopes of Ffrith Mountain.

Continue on the rising path which becomes less steep higher up with views left into the long sweeping valleys which cut into Moel Famau's eastern slopes. At a junction of paths turn left up towards the summit with conifer plantations to your left.

3. From the Jubilee Tower walk almost due east past the triangulation pillar to cross a stile in the fence. Follow a descending path which is steep at first before the angle eases as you walk along the rounded crest of a broad ridge. Lower down the path drops steeply again to join a farm track.

Turn right along the track crossing a stream with a deep valley

Looking down the wooded eastern slopes of Moel Famau

on the right with the wooded slopes of Moel Famau rising 600 feet at its head. Turn left across the field and walk parallel to the stream until you reach a fingerpost (level with the edge of woods on the right) directing you half-right over a rounded ridge in the field to a second fingerpost beside oak trees further on. Walk straight ahead, soon with a fence on the left and another steep sided valley on the right to cross a second stream.

Turn left on the signed path to a ladder stile in the fence corner (ignoring a stile into the trees on the right). Walk ahead by the fence on a good path to a stile on the left into fields again. Bear right through a small field to a stile into a short green lane. Turn left down a track and follow it as it bends right. Follow the track down to a lane.

Turn right along the lane then left in a few yards to return to Loggerheads Country Park.

Loggerheads &
Maeshafn

Distance: *4³/₄ or 7³/₄ miles*

An interesting and varied walk through mixed woodland and open countryside including a moderate ascent to Moel Findeg with its commanding views. Options for a shorter walk are included and a number of pubs are passed en-route.

Start: There is room for a few cars in a small layby on the A494 Mold to Ruthin road partway down the hill between Cadole and Loggerheads. *Grid ref: 202 626 (Landranger 116/117, Explorer 265).*

The walk

1. On the same side of the road as the layby, follow the signed footpath into the woods soon passing a quarry on the left.

After a crossing stile pass outbuildings and bear left along a driveway. Keep left at the next junction following the driveway towards the buildings of the Colomendy Outdoor Education Centre. Just before wooden buildings at a junction in the driveway, bear right, first on a tarmac road, then where this swings right, on a footpath passing large 'Swiss-style' buildings on the right. Climb a stile ahead and cross a field to enter woods by a second stile. Follow the good path ahead through the trees. Continue for about ¹/₂ mile passing through the 'Aberduna Nature Reserve'.

After passing a house on the left ('Bryn Tirion Cottage'), bear left at a T junction and follow the access track to a lane. Turn left up the lane to the edge of Maeshafn. (For a shorter walk continue into the village passing the 'Miner's Arms' on the right and continue from point 3.)

Maeshafn owes its origins to lead mining. Mines in the area date back to at least the eighteenth century with a peak in activity during the nineteenth century, although lead is known to have been mined in the locality since the Middle Ages. Most of the old buildings in the village originated as miners' cottages or public houses when the village would have had a far larger population.

2. Immediately after the drive to 'Hafn Deg Maeshafn' on the left, turn sharp right onto a track signed to 'Pentre Cerrig Mawr'. In a few hundred yards (ignoring the first stile in the fence on the left) bear left over a stile beside a large metal gate. Follow a good footpath through young birch woods for almost ½ mile.

At a junction take the path directly ahead which follows the edge of the woods as a gravel track before becoming a footpath again. Follow the path ignoring a left fork. This eventually steepens and drops to a track beside two houses. Turn left, then left again at a T junction with a second track. Follow the gently rising track overhung by trees for about ½ mile.

Just before a house bear right on a path which rises up the bank, then runs above the road. Meet the road by a fingerpost. Cross over here and take the signed footpath opposite. Follow the narrow footpath through the first small field to a stile in the far corner. After the stile turn right along the wall to the next stile beside a cottage on the right. In the following field continue straight ahead beside the right-hand fence under power lines. At the end of the fence keep straight ahead through the open field with hawthorn bushes on the left. Keep to the left of a rise in the field to reach a stile in a crossing fence. If there is no stile here you are probably too far to the right, turn left and you should soon find it.

Walk diagonally through the next field to a stile in the far corner. Go over the stile and keep to the right-hand field edge passing an empty cottage to enter the next field through a gateway. In the far right corner go over the stile and turn left to cross a second stile in a few yards. Drop down a bank and keep beside the fence on the left. A stile immediately before a house leads onto an access track. Follow this into Maeshafn where you will find the 'Miner's Arms'.

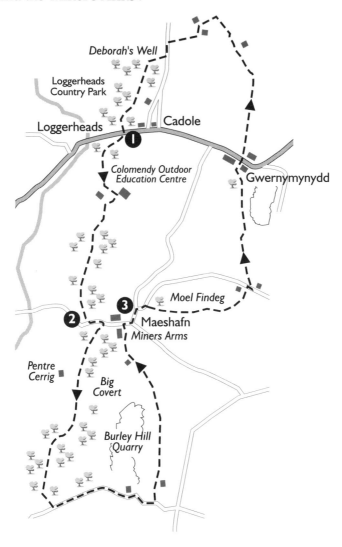

81

3. Turn right at the road and at the road junction turn left. Take the next minor lane on the right and in a few yards bear right into 'Moel Findeg Local Nature Reserve'. Follow the obvious footpath which makes its way to the summit of Moel Findeg which has surprisingly extensive views for such a modest hill.

Moel Findeg was saved from quarrying operations several years ago by funds raised locally to buy the land, thus ensuring its future access.

The grassy summit ridge is one of the best vantage points in the area. The view is dominated to the west by the forests and ridges of Moel Famau with the smooth green fields of Foel Fenlli and Moel Eithinen to the left. Moel Gyw and Moel Llanfair rise again beyond the gap which carries the A494 between Mold and Ruthin, while to the north the range continues to the rounded bulk of Moel y Parc.

Climb the stile by the information board and walk along the ridge. At its eastern end bear half-right down past a power line post and to the left of a small group of stunted pine trees, then walk ahead down the field to a gate in the far corner. Go through the gate and make your way along the field edge past a farm and pool to the lane.

Turn right along the lane and in about 50 yards turn sharp left onto a good farm track by 'Haulfryn'. Follow the track past small quarries on the right until a stile is reached in the wall to the left. Climb over the stile and bear half-right through the field with a quarry in the next field to the right. A stile in the lower wall leads down a wooded slope to a road in Gwernymynydd ('Llys Enfys'). Turn right to the main road with 'The Rainbow Inn' to the right. Cross the road and follow a good access track opposite for a little over 1/2 mile.

Just before a large gate leading to a house, bear left over a stile and keep beside the wall on the right. Pass through a gate into a second field, turn left along the fence and look for a stile in the fence partway down the field. Go over the stile and walk through the centre of the field (directly towards Moel Famau) to a stile in the far wall. Bear left through a small field to join an enclosed path between gardens which leads to a track by houses. Turn left along the track and bear right by 'Pathside' onto a short enclosed footpath which soon leads into fields again. Go ahead through the centre of the field to a stile in the far left corner which leads onto the road.

Cross the road and the stile opposite and turn left along the wood edge to 'Deborah's Well'.

An engraved plaque here tells the story of Deborah, who is said to have lived at the nearby settlement of Conlan in the sixteenth century. Conlan predated Gwernaffield which developed later as a mining settlement. When Cholera came to the area, Deborah arranged for those not affected to be moved to higher ground. Although she did not understand that Cholera was spread through the water supply, it had been noted that people living on higher ground were less likely to be affected.

On the summit of Moel Findeg with a view to Moel Famau

A hospital was built and all went well until the Cholera spread to those under Deborah's care. She was accused of cursing those she had cared for and sentenced by the village elders to burning. The wooden hospital was set on fire killing all inside, including Deborah.

Just beyond the well turn right onto a signed footpath which makes a short rise through the trees to enter a small field. Walk ahead along the field edge to enter woods again and turn left almost immediately onto a good path. After a stile continue on the obvious path which eventually curves left through a small clearing to a large gate on the left. Don't go through the gate (unless you are visiting the 'Colomendy Arms'), turn right along a footpath back into the trees again. Cross a stile and continue to a T junction. Turn left here and follow the broad path back to the road.

Following Offa's Dyke Path below Foel Fenlli (walk 14)

Moel Famau & Foel Fenlli

Distance: *4¹/₂ or 7³/₄ miles*

A strenuous route visiting two well known summits in the Clwydian Range. An unusual approach to Moel Famau is followed by easy walking along the ridge and a visit to one of the best preserved hillforts in the range. Parts of the route are quite strenuous but views are magnificent from the higher ground.

Start: Begin at the pay and display forest car park situated 1 mile along the narrow lane which leaves the A494 Mold to Ruthin road, about ¹/₂ mile west of Loggerheads.
Grid ref: 172 611 (Landranger 116, Explorer 265).

The walk

1. There are two parking areas and a WC block here. From the car park entrance walk ahead through the barrier (WC block to the left) and where the road swings left almost immediately, fork right. This track soon turns sharp right into one of the parking areas, but a footpath continues ahead. Take this path and bear right at a fork in about 100 yards. Make a short rise to a forest road at a sharp bend and take the higher left-hand track.

Just as the track begins to level there is a fork; keep right here and in a further 250 yards at a second fork, keep right again. Follow this descending forest road close to the edge of the woods on the right passing a house away to the right. A little further on (120 yards) bear right down off the track onto a path indicated by a waymark. Follow this narrower path until you begin to drop

85

into the valley and you get glimpses of Moel Famau ahead. Continue until a way mark on a low post directs you right steeply down through a felled area to stile. Climb the stile, bear left to the corner of a fence, cross the stream and continue beside the fence on your right. Where the fence bends right, continue straight ahead passing a fingerpost and waymark at the edge of woods on the left.

Bear half-left now through a large field with Moel Famau directly ahead. The right of way runs mid-way between woods on the left and a stream on the right. Further on, walk nearer to the stream until you meet a path which crosses it. Turn right, cross the stream and follow a path which soon runs beside woods on the left. Shortly there is a signed path on the left ('Moel Famau'). Turn left here and

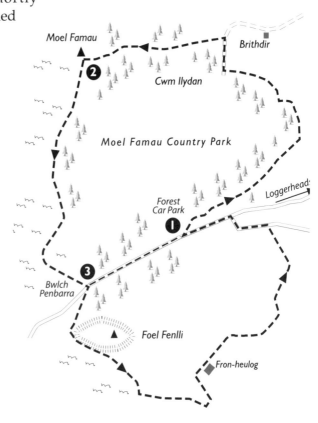

rise steeply through the trees onto the crest of a rounded ridge which rises directly to the summit of Moel Famau.

The ruined tower which crowns the summit was built in 1810 to commemorate the 50th year of the reign of King George III. A ceremony, attended by over 3,000 people who made the long walk to the summit, was held on October 25th and included 'most of the nobility and gentry in Denbighshire and Flintshire'.

Designed in the Egyptian style, it was originally intended to reach a height of 150 feet. The plans were never fully carried out however, and the structure that was built collapsed in 1862 following a series of storms. Attempts were made to restore the tower in 1887 for Queen Victoria's Golden Jubilee but renovations were a failure and the present structure is all that remains.

All that is of interest here today are the four engraved panoramas which depict highlights from one of the most extensive views in northeast Wales.

2. Leave the tower at its southern corner taking the signed Offa's Dyke Path which heads due south along the broad ridge with conifer woods to the left and an extensive view over the Vale of Clwyd to your right. Continue to Bwlch Penbarra crossed by the hill road below Foel Fenlli (about $1^1/_2$ mile).

3. To shorten the walk turn left here and follow the road back to point **1**. Alternatively, bear diagonally-right up the steep slopes of Foel Fenlli following the Offa's Dyke Path signs which take you around the western perimeter of the Iron Age hillfort crowning the summit.

This is one of the most impressive hillforts on the Clwydian Range. The earthworks, which completely enclose the hilltop, rise to 35 feet above the outer ditch in places. Within the defences, remains of over 30 hut circles, along with fragments of fifth century Romano-British pottery and coins have been found. Two in-turned entrances originally gave access to the fort and a wooden palisade would have topped the ramparts.

At over 1,600 feet, Foel Fenlli commands a wide panorama, particularly to the west where the smooth hillsides drop steeply to the Vale of Clwyd. The little market town of Ruthin fits comfortably into this agricultural landscape, while further west the flatness of the Denbigh Moors contrasts sharply with the serrated peaks of Snowdonia which peep over the horizon. To the north and south, the graceful curves of the Clwydians rise and fall, while to the east lies the Cheshire Plain.

Follow the contouring path for about 1/2 mile. This is marked by squat posts carrying the Offa's Dyke Path waymarkers.

On the southern side of Foel Fenlli, above a belt of conifers descend steeply down to the right as signed. At the bottom of the slope cross two stiles close together and walk beside woods to a third stile which takes you into grazing fields. Bear half-left down a wide grassy valley to a stile to the right of a small wood. Cross the stile, pass the wood and continue beside the wall to the far corner of the field.

Leave Offa's Dyke Path which bears right here, instead turn left over a stile and follow a faint farm track which rises to 'Fron-heulog', a large stone-built farmhouse on the hillside. Keep to the left of the farm and join a track which rises steadily over the hillside beside walls for about 1 1/4 miles.

Drop to a lane beside a cottage, turn left and at a T junction turn left again to complete the walk.

Foel Fenlli from Llanferres

Distance: *5 miles*

A strenuous route through farmland and along a section of the Offa's Dyke Path to the shoulder of Foel Fenlli with its Iron Age hillfort and spectacular views into the Vale of Clwyd. Footpaths are good throughout.

Start: There are two possible starting points: a small layby on the A494 *(Grid ref: 187 598)* or the 'Druid Inn' at Llanferres *(Grid ref: 189 604).* Please only use this start if you are visiting the pub and ask permission to park before you start the walk. *(Landranger 116, Explorer 265).*

The walk

1. From the layby cross the road and walk back towards Llanferres (north) for about 350 yards. Cross a stile up to the left which leads into sloping fields and bear half-right up the field to a stile in crossing hedgeline. Continue uphill beside the fence to a second stile on the right. Cross the stile and turn left to go through a large gate.

(Alternatively, from the 'Druid Inn' turn right up 'Rectory Lane' and follow the rising lane to its end where it enters the gardens of cottages. Walk past the cottages towards a stile visible ahead. Don't cross the stile, instead turn right through a large field gate.)

Rise steeply by the hedge to a small gate on the left. Go through the gate and walk ahead beside the left-hand hedge line.

Pass a farm on the left and go through a gate ahead. Walk beside the hedge to the next gate. Go through this gate and cut across the field to a small gate about 50 yards left of the right-hand corner. In the next field aim for pine trees visible ahead and as you approach the woods walk beside them (on your left).

This is a narrow belt of pines and before you reach the end of them, bear half-left through the trees on a narrow footpath to emerge in a sloping field. Follow the footpath which bears half-left down the field to an unsurfaced farm access track.

Go right along the track and where this turns right through the wall (towards a farm high up on the hillside), keep ahead beside the wall to a large gate in the corner. Go through the gate and beside the woods on the left. Shortly, at the end of the trees, bear left to a stile in the corner of the field.

2. Cross the stile and turn right to walk beside the wall. This is now the Offa's Dyke Path. Pass woods on the right and continue ahead up a wide grassy valley to a stile in the fence on the skyline beside conifers up to the right. (The right of way goes almost to

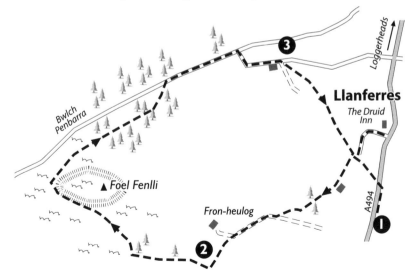

Foel Fennli and Bwlch Penbarra from the north

the top corner of the field, then bears right to the stile just mentioned).

Cross the stile and walk beside the conifers to cross two more stiles close together. You now have a steep climb ahead up the heather-clad slopes of Foel Fenlli with widening views left over the Vale of Clwyd.

At a squat marker post the worst of the climb is over and the path splits. The recommended route is the Offa's Dyke Path which contours leftwards from here but a narrower footpath continues the climb to the summit of Foel Fenlli. For the Offa's Dyke Path follow the contouring path which makes a slight descent further around the hillside near the lower earthworks of the hillfort which surround the summit, before continuing to contour.

On the western slopes the view is at its best taking in almost the entire Vale of Clwyd sweeping north to the sea at Rhyl and Towyn.

Keep following the ODP until you round the hillside and can see down to the parking area at Bwlch Penbarra. The path heads diagonally down to the bwlch.

At the bottom of the slope don't continue to the road, instead turn right immediately after a small pond and cross a parking area to a gravel forest track beyond a large gate. Walk down the track to eventually join the road.

Turn right along the road passing the forest car park and picnic area (WC) to a lane on the right (just under ¹/₂ mile).

3. Turn right here and walk along the lane to a cottage, 'Tyn y Groesffordd', on the right beside a signed bridleway. Turn right immediately after the house, but don't follow the bridleway (unsurfaced track) bear left immediately over a stile into a large field. Walk ahead through the centre of the field until two sets of farm buildings come into view. Head to the right of the right-hand buildings. Go through gates adjacent to the buildings to join a farm access track. Follow the track ahead and where this forks keep left. Follow the track to a gate, go through the gate but don't go through the next gate immediately ahead, instead bear to the left and walk by the fence on the right to a stile in the right-hand corner. Cross the stile and contour the following field rising slightly and passing above houses on the left to a large gate in the far corner. Turn left through the gate and either bear left past cottages to return to the 'Druid Inn' or turn right over the stile for the layby.

Bryn Alyn &
Moel Findeg

Distance: *7 miles*

An excellent walk with superb views of the central Clwydian Range throughout. Good footpaths are used to explore steep ground on the limestone escarpment of Bryn Alyn and the woods and pastures of Nercwys Mountain. Moel Findeg, one of the best viewpoints in the area is also included.

Start: Free parking is available in a layby on the A494 Mold to Ruthin road just south of the village of Llanferres. *Grid ref: 187 598 (Landranger 117, Explorer 265).*

The walk

1. From the layby take the signed footpath on the right which follows a farm track to a metal bridge over Afon Alyn (not the footbridge a few yards to the left). Cross the river and bear right along the bank, then go left to a gate in the far corner. Continue ahead in the next field to a stile in the fence, with stepping stones and a small footbridge over the stream. The well worn path continues ahead over metal railings and soon below crags on the left. Continue with the woods of Big Covert on the left ignoring a footpath on the left to pass two houses near a T junction with an unsurfaced track. Turn left up the track.

As the track levels (about ½ mile) ignore a signed footpath on the left and as you approach a cottage a little further on look for a stile on the right by a fingerpost ('Bryn Alyn'). Turn sharp right over the stile and follow the path as it climbs diagonally up the hillside.

Limestone pavement on Bryn Alyn

You are soon able to see into the large quarry across the valley and as the path levels and you begin to contour, superb views open out of the Clwydian ridge to the west. The conical top of Foel Fenlli dominates and can be seen alongside Moel Famau with Moel Gyw and Moel Llanfair to the south of the Clwyd Gate.

Continue to contour until the path levels at a small field on the right. Keep ahead for another 200 yards or so to reach a stile in the fence. Cross the stile and continue ahead to a grass path/track. Turn left and rise with the track to enter a small hollow below crags with one or two mounds from mining explorations down to the left.

To the right there is small example of a feature known as a limestone pavement. These are quite rare in Wales being most common in the north of England. They are formed when the bedding planes of carboniferous limestone are exposed and then dissolved by the affect of mild acids present in rain water. This forms the distinctive fissures known as 'grikes'.

Continue along the track which soon bears left out of the hollow. At the top of the rise keep ahead on the track to pass through grazing fields to a lane.

2. Turn left along the lane for about 35 yards before turning right down the access track to 'Fron Deg'. Where the track bears left to the house, climb the stile ahead into fields. Walk through a small field then a larger one keeping to the right edge. Before the next stile ahead turn left across the field to a stile in the corner. Cross the stile and keep ahead close to the right-hand field edge in a large field to a stile in the far corner partly hidden by gorse bushes. Keep ahead through two more fields to a lane opposite a house 'Coed Bach'.

Cross the lane, go through the gates and pass to the left of the house to a gate and stile which lead onto a track running along the woodland edge. At the end of the track go over a stile by a

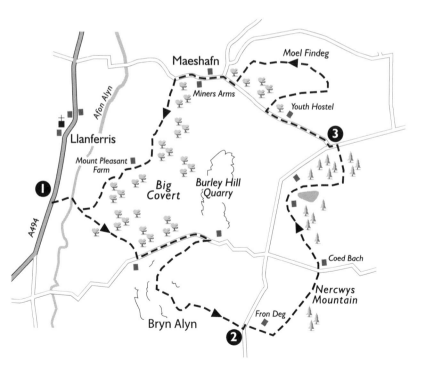

gate and pass a barn on the left to a stile in the fence. Go ahead through the following small fields to a stile in the fence on the left below power cables (pines on the right). After the stile bear right through a grazing field. At an access track turn right for a few yards to cross a stile beside the gate to a wooden bungalow. Follow a path through a small wood to a stile which leads into fields again. Bear right to the next stile behind a belt of gorse, then half-right through rough grass to a stile into a garden. Go ahead through the garden and into woods.

Pass a small marshy woodland pool on the right and continue on the obvious path through the trees. Follow the path down through the woods. Ignore the first path junction, continuing to a second junction near the edge of the woods with a farm ahead. Turn left to the road.

3. Turn left then right into 'Ffordd Maeshafn'. Walk along the lane past a building on the right. Take the next signed footpath on the right beside the 'Moel Findeg' sign opposite a driveway. Follow the main footpath ahead through the trees and where the path splits at a fingerpost keep right soon entering fields by a stile. The path continues ahead past a small pond which may be dry in the summer and between gorse bushes to a gap in the fence, then ahead through the centre of a second field. Immediately before the next stile and gate with ruins beyond, turn left up the bank and continue beside the fence on the right. Where the fence bends right, bear left and walk up to Moel Findeg (the right-hand and most pointed of the two hilltops ahead).

In clear conditions this is a superb viewpoint giving panoramas both eastwards over the Cheshire Plain and Wirral to Liverpool's waterfront and west to include much of the Clwydian Range. To the south lie the moors above World's End. In very clear conditions I have seen the pyramidal peak of Snowdon through the gap between Moel Famau and Foel Fenlli due west of here.

Moel Findeg Nature Reserve was created in 1999 from land acquired by Denbighshire County Council supported by funds raised locally to ensure the area was not disfigured by further quarrying operations.

Walk along the grassy ridge and over the stile near the 'Moel Findeg' sign. Follow the descending path keeping left where this forks near a small pond over to the left. The path soon passes through what remains of the heather which once covered Moel Findeg, with views down to Maeshafn and Moel Famau beyond. At the lane turn right and at the next road junction go left into Maeshafn.

Walk along the road past the seventeenth century 'Miner's Arms' and out of the village on a descending lane. After a signed path on the right to 'Loggerheads' the lane steepens and in another 150 yards or so there is a signed path on the left. Go through the gate and before the second gate turn left onto a footpath. This climbs gently through woods.

At an access road bear right along the road and where this swings right, bear left over a cattle grid on the track to 'Mount Pleasant Farm'.

Follow the track to the farm and just before the house bear left up the bank to two gates. Ignore the signed footpath through the left-hand gate, instead, go through the right-hand gate and turn right along the right-hand field edge. Bear left along the bottom edge of the field below a wooded bank to a stile in the far corner. Cut through the centre of the following field to bend left along the bottom of a scrub covered bank. The line of the right of way keeps tight against the bank, then a stone wall in the scrub on the left. Follow this path to the stepping stones used at the beginning of the walk. Turn right to return to the start.

Moel Gyw from Llanarmon-yn-Iâl

Distance: *5¹/₄ or 7¹/₂ miles*

A route which takes in some of the lesser known summits in the Clwydian Range. Excellent footpaths used by Offa's Dyke Path link with quieter trails to create a walk centred on the ancient village of Llanarmon-yn-Iâl. Walking is quite strenuous in parts, but excellent views can be enjoyed from the ridge.

Start: A free car park has been created at Pistyll Gwyn Quarry near Llanarmon-yn-Iâl. This is situated on the B5430 about 1 mile north of the village.

Grid ref: 189 573 (Landranger 116, Explorer 265).

The walk

1. Turn right along the lane and in about 50 yards, opposite a narrow lane on the right, turn left onto a footpath enclosed by hedges which leads down to Afon Alyn. Cross the footbridge over the river and continue on the footpath to a quiet lane.

At the lane take the track opposite to 'Cyfnant Uchaf'. After about 100 yards turn right over a stile and rise up the track to a house on the hillside. Bear right just before the house and walk around the garden. Pass a solitary tree on the skyline ahead and a little further on, over the brow of the hill, turn half-left down a steeply sloping field which drops into an attractive little valley. A stile on the left at the bottom of the slope confirms that you are still on the right of way.

Cross the stile and go ahead to a second stile in the fence on the right (about 120 yards). Turn half-left through the following fields aiming for a grey farmhouse below a conifer wood. As you approach the house cross a stile in the fence on the left and turn right beside the fence. A stile immediately after the outbuildings leads onto a path which makes a short rise to a forest track. Turn sharp right onto this and follow it up through the trees, keeping left at a fork.

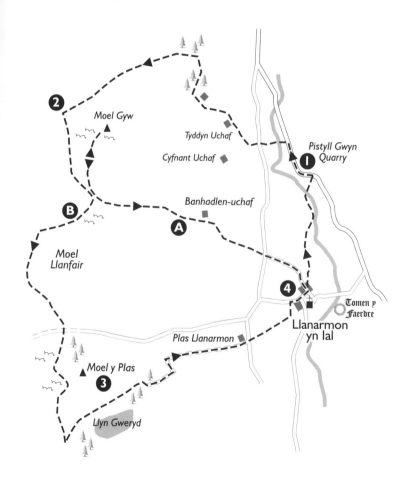

Moel Gyw from Bryn Alyn

At the top of the rise keep ahead to a stile which leads into fields once more. Walk across a small field to a stile into a second conifer wood. The path bears half-left at first then turns right (yellow markers on trees at the time of writing). In 100-150 yards or so look for a path on the left (also marked by yellow paint on the trees). Turn left onto this path and rise gently through the trees to a stile on the edge of the woods. Cross the stile and walk ahead contouring the hillside with a fine view rightwards to Moel Eithinen and Foel Fenlli.

This field is large and at the time of writing there is a crossing fence at the far side but no stile. Cross the fence here and continue contouring to a gate in the far corner. Go through the gate and walk ahead beside the fence to a second gate where you will join the Offa's Dyke Path.

2. Turn left here and follow the broad path which contours the hillside and gives wide views across the Vale of Clwyd.

Where the path forks just before the next pass, turn sharp left and follow a narrow signed footpath ('Moel Gyw') up to an agricultural road. Turn left for a few yards to a stone ('AONB Moel Gyw') which marks the start of a footpath up through the heather to the triangulation pillar on the summit of Moel Gyw.

This little excursion is well worth the effort as the panorama from the summit is one of the finest on the Clwydian Range. The view to the west is dominated by the Vale of Clwyd, with its rich green fields and oak lined hedgerows. The focal point is the market town of Ruthin, built on a rise adjacent to the castle and arranged around St. Peter's Square.

The most prominent feature from here is undoubtedly the tall broach spire of St. Peter's church, added during restoration work carried out in the mid-nineteenth century. The main fabric of the church is fourteenth century and originally housed a small community of monks. Perhaps because of this, parts of the church were demolished after the Dissolution. Inside is a fine carved and panelled roof said to have been presented by Henry VII in gratitude to the men of North Wales who fought beside him on Bosworth Field in 1485.

The rest of the town is a pleasant mix of period styles with several buildings dating back to the fifteenth and sixteenth centuries. Of particular note is the Old Court House, originally built in 1401 with remains of the town gibbet still visible.

The nearby castle was originally built in the thirteenth century during the reign of Edward I. Parts of the original fabric remain but the majority is modern and is now a hotel.

Edward I gave Ruthin to the Grey family following his conquest of Wales in 1283 and it was still in their ownership when Owain Glyndŵr burned much of the town in 1401. Glyndŵr's famous rebellion was triggered by a minor quarrel with Lord Grey over land near Glyndyfrdwy in the Dee valley.

Retrace your steps to the AONB stone and walk ahead along the track for about 100 yards to a point where there is a broad footpath on the right and a large, round boulder immediately opposite on the left (probably a boundary stone separating the parishes of Llanarmon-yn-Iâl, Llanfair Dyffryn and Llanbedr).

Looking north to Foel Fenlli from the lower slopes of Moel Gyw

Here you have two options. For a shorter round continue from paragraph **A**, or for a longer walk go to paragraph **B**.

A. Bear left past the boulder on a narrow footpath through the heather to a ladder stile. Enter grazing fields, and go ahead to a second stile beside a gate. Turn left along the fence now and walk along the crest of a rounded ridge with an attractive little valley to your left and Llanarmon-yn-Iâl immediately ahead.

As you begin to drop, bear half-right to a stile. Cross the stile, then keep ahead down a small field towards a farmhouse. After a stile, head down through the bracken to a second stile. Go down the bank then bear left before the garden by a stream. Before a pond go right to join an access road leading to the farm ('Banhadlen Uchaf'). Turn left along the road and where it bears right, a stile straight ahead marks the field path back to Llanarmon-yn-Iâl. Go ahead through the field to enter a lane beside a small chapel. Continue straight ahead along the lane to Llanarmon-yn-Iâl. About 100 yards before 'The Raven Inn' turn left onto a signed footpath passing in front of 'Brydal Cottage'. Continue from point **4**.

B. Turn right onto the broad path and at the fingerpost turn sharp left on the signed Offa's Dyke Path. At the end of the path cross the stile and turn right to follow a descending agricultural road. A few yards after the road swings right, look for the signed Offa's Dyke Path on the left. This follows a broad track which contours the hillside to the next pass.

Cross a farm road here and take the path almost opposite—a continuation of the Offa's Dyke Path which rises to Moel-y-Plas. At the top of the rise follow the path ahead through the heather and beside the fence until a stile leads into grazing fields. Turn right for about 35 yards, then bear left down a sloping field. Cross a stile at the bottom of the slope, turn left immediately and cross a second stile in the corner at the edge of woods. Bear right now through a large field with woods on the right at first, then the waters of Llyn Gweryd. The right of way slowly veers away from the woods on the right aiming towards pines on the skyline ahead and rising above the lake.

3. When you reach the pines look for a stile in the fence on the right (about two thirds of the way along). Cross this and make a short descent to a farm track. Turn left here and follow the track down to a T junction beyond a large farmhouse on the left (about ³/₄ mile).

Take the signed field path directly ahead which bears half-left through the centre of the field to a stile in the corner. Go ahead in the following two fields to enter a modern housing estate ('Maes Iâl') by an enclosed path. Take the first road on the left, and at the T junction turn right into the village.

Llanarmon-yn-Iâl sits in a quiet valley on the banks of the Alyn; its handful of cottages and pub gathered tightly around the ancient church of St. Garmon, founded by St. Germanus who has many associations in this part of Wales.

Iâl (pronounced 'yale'), meaning a 'hilly area', describes the locality well and became the name of the medieval commote which included much of the southern Clwydians as far south as the River Dee. It was also adopted as the surname of one local family whose most prominent son, Elihu Yale, became the benefactor of Yale University.

During the eighteenth century lead mining in the hills to the east enabled many locals to supplement their income or to leave the land completely for a life of toil below ground.

Pass the post Office and village shop on the left and opposite the church turn left immediately before 'The Raven Inn'. In about 100 yards look for a signed footpath on the right by 'Brydal Cottage'.

4. Walk past the front of the cottage to a stile which leads onto a short path enclosed by hedges. Turn left and at the end of the footpath cross the stile into fields. Go ahead now through the centre of the field (in the direction of Pistyll Gwyn Quarry on the hillside ahead) to cross a stile in the far fence. Follow the path ahead through the next two fields and immediately as you enter the third field, bear right around the field edge to a stile in the far corner by a caravan.

Cross the stile and cut through a small field to where a footbridge leads over Afon Alyn. Beyond the bridge, follow a track for about 30 yards before bearing left onto a narrow footpath which leads to a lane. Turn left along the lane to return to the car park.

Llanarmon-yn-Iâl & Eryrys

Distance: *5½ miles*

A walk exploring the lesser-known limestone hills separated from the main Clwydian ridge by the Alyn valley. The route includes the ancient village of Llanarmon-yn-Iâl along with the tiny mining village of Eryrys. Footpaths are generally good and views of Moel Famau and the southern Clwydian Range are superb for much of the walk.

Start: A new free car park has been created at Pistyll Gwyn Quarry near Llanarmon-yn-Iâl. This is more suitable for walkers than trying to park in the village where space is very limited. It is situated on the B5430 about 1 mile north of Llanarmon-yn-Iâl. *Grid ref: 189 573 (Landranger 116/117, Explorer 265).*

The walk

1. Turn left out of the car park and follow the signed 'Permissive Path' which runs along the grass verge close to the road, then veers left uphill by a rockface into the trees. After a right turn bear left along the edge of the trees with fields and a house on the right. After a rise left a stile leads into a small field with the quarry a few yards away on the left. Walk ahead across the field to the far corner, then by the fence to a stile in the far fence with a fingerpost beyond. Turn left here and follow a rising path with the quarry close by on the left.

Where the footpath enters a field, keep ahead to a gate in the far fence which leads beside 'Bryn-y-gloch' to a quiet lane.

Turn right along the lane (ignore a turning to 'Fron Cottage Farm' immediately on the right) and keep right at a fork in about 30 yards. Follow the rising lane.

The lane ends at a gate ('Tan-y-Marian' on the left) which leads into open grazing fields. Go through the gate and in a few yards bear right on a rising diagonal footpath. At the top of the rise the path swings right, then left. A little further on when a gate comes into view about 100 yards ahead, bear left down through gorse bushes to a stile over a wall ahead. Go ahead through the following field to the corner to join an old unsurfaced lane.

Turn right along the lane and in about 200 yards where the lane levels turn left through a gateway and cross a stile. Walk ahead initially, then curve leftwards before the fence to follow a path which heads up towards the skyline. As you reach the highest point you walk beside flat limestone outcrops, a feature known as 'limestone pavements'.

Limestone pavements are quite rare particularly in Wales and are most common in Yorkshire, Cumbria and north Lancashire, but one or two examples are to be found here in North Wales. They are formed when the bedding planes of carboniferous limestone become exposed producing large slabs or 'pavements' of rock. Further erosion from the mild acids found in rain water dissolves the rock slab to form the distinctive fissures, known as 'grikes'. These shelter a rich variety of unique flora and fauna which are not found beyond the area of the pavement. Sadly a fashion for using water-worn limestone from limestone pavements to build rockeries and ornamental gardens has resulted in the damage and destruction of many of these features.

Continue over the highest point (Bryn Alyn) and follow the line of the rocks down to join an unsurfaced track in a hollow. Turn right along the track and follow it as it curves leftwards out of the hollow to pass through grazing fields. Follow the track for about 350 yards and as you approach a stile in the fence on the left (just before overhead cables), turn right across the large

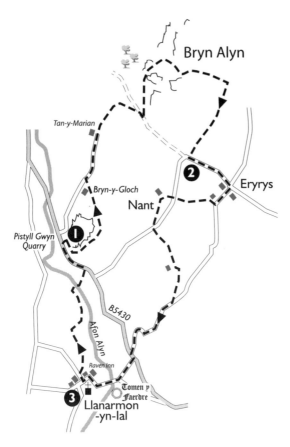

open field towards a rocky cutting. Immediately before the cutting turn right along a faint grass track for about 25 yards and where this bends right, turn left through gorse bushes to stone steps in the wall. In the next field locate a ladder stile in the wall over to the right which should soon be visible and make your way through the gorse which occupies much of the field. Cross the stile and in the following field keep half-left through more scrub where the path is not visible. Further on you can look down to a lane where there is an old shed immediately adjacent to the road. Head for this and join the lane by a stile behind the shed.

The view west to Moel Gyw from Bryn Alyn

2. Turn left along the lane and at the crossroads turn right to walk through Eryrys passing the 'Sun Inn' and further on at the edge of the village an old chapel on the right.

Eryrys is a quite rural hamlet with just the sound of children playing and the odd car to break the silence; but during the nineteenth century, when it lay at the centre of a thriving lead mining industry, its population, including nearby Graianrhyd, grew to over 1,000 and the surrounding countryside would have throbbed with the sound and activity of mining. Many buildings which are now private houses would have originated as inns to supply the miners working nearby.

Lead mining has a long history in this area with the Romans said to be among the earliest prospectors. By the time of Edward I mining was obviously well established as local miners were recruited to work in new mines in southern Britain.

Look for a stile on the right by caravans soon after the old chapel. Turn right here to cross a small field to a stile over the wall. Keep straight ahead now in a larger field passing beneath overhead cables to a stile in the far fence.

In clear conditions there are distant views left to the Berwyn and Aran mountains with the Clwydian ridge nearer at hand to the right.

In the following field keep ahead again for a few yards then look for a stile in the fence on the left. Turn left over the stile and walk down through an area of waste—known as 'silver sand'; a by-product of lead mining—to a rough track and turn right. Follow the track, ignoring two right forks, to a lane. Turn left along the lane for a few yards then right on a footpath towards a large square stone tower associated with mining in the area.

This little valley, known as Nant, lay at the centre of a thriving lead mining industry during the nineteenth century and this seemingly out-of-place structure is the remains of a large engine house used to pump water from the lead mines. Flooding became an increasing problem as the mines became deeper.

At the next junction turn left down a track to reach the lane again. Directly opposite, take the signed footpath up the bank to a stile in the wall and into fields. Walk directly through the field to a stile in the far wall. After the stile bear half-right to walk beside the lower fence passing overgrown mounds from nearby mines on the left. At the end of the field pass crumbling ruins on the right and head towards a farm directly ahead. About 50 yards before the farm turn left and in another 50 yards or so turn right through a gate and stile to cross a small field to a lane (the farm should now be down to your right). Turn left along the lane and continue to the road. Turn right down the road to the B5430. Turn left here then right at the Llanarmon-yn-Iâl sign.

Down by the river (Afon Alyn) look to your left where you will see the mound—partly defended by a natural crag—of a motte and bailey castle. Motte and baileys were built during the eleventh and twelfth centuries either by the Normans themselves or the by Welsh copying the Norman style.

At the top of the rise you enter the little village of Llanarmon-yn-

Iâl; its collection of stone houses and village pub gathered around the plain double-naved church. The dedication is to Saint Garmon, better known as Germanus, the fifth century Bishop of Auxerre. He seems to have thought nothing of raising arms against his enemies or those of the church.

The local connection is a famous battle said to have taken place near Mold in which the local British forces enjoyed an easily won victory over a heathen mob of Saxons and Picts know as the 'Alleluia Victory'. Germanus is said to have raised a British force to face the Saxons who were pushing west into what is now North Wales. Encouraged by Germanus, the British are said to have advanced shouting "Alleluia"— 'praise Jah' or 'God', a call which so terrified their enemies that they turned and fled to be cut down by British swords or drown in the nearby river. Germanus claimed a miraculous God-given victory!

Fanciful stuff. The story stands in stark contrast to the more sober account of the Battle of Chester in which the British forces were slaughtered by a force of Northumbrians. With them perished over 1,000 monks from the nearby abbey at Bangor-is-y-coed who had turned out to pray for a British victory over the heathens.

3. Turn right immediately after 'The Raven Inn' and in 100 yards or so turn right onto a signed footpath. This leads beside 'Brydal Cottage' and onto an enclosed footpath between gardens. Turn left and at the end of the path cross a stile into fields. Bear half-right through the centre of the field (in the direction Pistyll Gwyn Quarry) to a stile in the fence. Follow the path ahead through two smaller fields and after the third stile bear right around the field edge to a stile in the far corner by caravans (river to the right).

Follow a footpath through a small field to where a footbridge leads over the river. Beyond the bridge, follow a track for about 30 yards before turning left onto a narrow footpath which soon leads to the road. Turn left along the road to return to the car park.

Graianrhyd

Distance: *7¹/₂ miles*

An excellent walk which combines craggy limestone escarpments and wide views of the Clwydian Range, with the flat moors of Llandegla and Llyn Cyfynwy. Paths are good throughout the walk which uses an assortment of bridleways and field paths.

Start: Begin the walk in Graianrhyd, a tiny hamlet situated on the B5430 partway between Llanarmon-yn-Iâl and Rhydtalog. Parking is very limited in the lane, one option being at the 'Rose and Crown Inn' but only with the landlord's permission. *Grid ref: 218 561 (Landranger 117, Explorer 256).*

The walk

1. From the car park of the 'Rose and Crown Inn' and with the pub on your right, cross the road and walk down the lane opposite. This soon curves right into 'Graianrhyd Farm' but the right of way continues ahead as a stony path which rises between fields for about ¹/₂ mile.

At a tarmac lane a stile almost opposite marks a permissive footpath which skirts a wet marshy area before rising leftwards a short distance to Llyn Cyfynwy on the high point ahead. Don't go too far to the right or you will miss the lake. Alternatively, a right of way also leads up to the lake but the path is in a poorer condition. This can be reached by turning left along the lane for 150 yards or so. The signed footpath is on the right on the bend (partly hidden at the time of writing). Go over the stile and walk straight up through the heather beside a crumbling stone wall to the shore of the lake.

The lake sits in a small hollow just below the highest point on this section of the moors. On calm days the water mirrors the wide sky so characteristic of the moors and the flat horizon contrasts with the shapely Clwydian Range out to the west.

The path goes right (anticlockwise) around the lake to pass near a chalet on the far side. From here turn right down the access

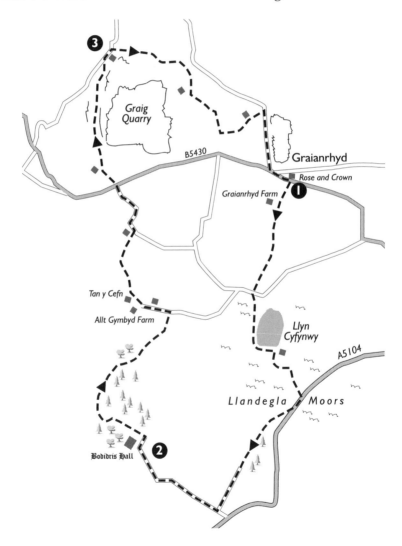

road away from the lake and down to the road (A5104). Turn right along the road for about 75 yards before bearing right onto a signed footpath. The right of way follows a track at first before bearing left over a stile just before a cattle grid and gate. A second stile leads into fields and the path continues ahead with the fence on the left.

After passing woods on the left a farm track is reached. Keep straight ahead ignoring the right fork. At the end of the track turn right at a T junction, signed to 'Bodidris Hall' and follow the lane up to the Hall.

2. Bear right with the drive past the front of the hall and at the end of the wall enclosing the rear of the building turn left onto a stony track. Follow the track into woods where you will often be accompanied by hundreds of young pheasants bred locally for shooting. Ignoring paths on both sides continue to a large gate across the track which leads into fields. Don't go through the gate, instead turn left over a stile just before the gate and walk ahead with the fence for 100 yards or so. At the corner of the fence bear half-right following a terraced path which rises gently to the top of a bank. Where the path levels and the Clwydian hills can be seen over to the left, curve half-right soon to walk beside a line of low limestone rocks on the right.

To your left you will see a grass bank running parallel to the rocks on your right. These are the exposed layers of limestone which are dipping down to the southeast. The layered nature of the rock causes this terracing which can be seen even more dramatically further north near Graig Quarry.

Continue straight ahead now to a stile in the fence which leads into an area of young trees. Pick your way through the trees straight ahead for about 500 yards before bearing half-right through a gap in the fence and diagonally across the adjacent field to a gate in the far (wire) fence. Go through the gate and turn right along the fence to a stile in the corner. Turn left after the stile and walk along the field edge to the lane.

Turn left and follow the lane to 'Allt Gymbyd Farm' caravan site. Turn right through a gate ('Tan-y-Cefn') immediately before the caravan site and follow a tarmac drive. Just before the house bear right up the bank on a signed path. Go through a gate and pass through the left-hand gap in the hedge immediately ahead. Walk through a small field passing to the right of an aerial and rising to pass through a second gap in the far hedge. Bear half-left after this down through the bushes to a stile in the fence. Cross a small field passing under power lines to an overgrown stile, then bear diagonally through the next field, with Moel Famau ahead, to a stile in the corner. Pass through an area of hawthorn and hazel bushes ahead to a stile which leads into an area of lorries and farm vehicles. Turn right and pass the house to reach a lane.

Turn left and follow the descending lane down to the road (B5430). Cross over and take the track opposite. Where this bears left to 'Pen-y-Llwyn', continue straight ahead on a footpath to a stile behind the house. Walk beside a stone wall on the right with widening views out to the left across the Alyn valley.

The southern hills of the Clwydian Range—Moel Gyw, Moel Llanfair, Moel-y-Plas and Moel y Waun—can now be seen across the Alyn valley with the village of Llanarmon-yn-Iâl at their feet.

Where the wall ends, continue ahead descending slightly to a grass shelf between limestone crags. This now climbs gently again to reach a high point between crags on the right and a ridge of limestone on the left.

Like the terraces seen earlier in the walk this stepped formation is the result of weathering of the inclined layers which are rising to the west and dipping to the east. There are one or two tiny limestone pavements where the top of the layers have been exposed and then dissolved by rain water to form the distinctive fissures known as 'grikes. Where weathering has cut at right angles to the layers, crags are the result which can be seen to your right.

3. A little further on the path drops to a stile which leads into a lane beside houses. Turn right and follow the rising lane to a signed bridleway on the right. Turn right here and follow the track until, just after a small pool on the right, there is a fork. Bear right here and follow the main track until it bends right towards a farm. Turn left over a stile in the fence and pass caravans to a gate in the far corner of the field. Go through the gate and walk ahead a few yards to a stone and metal stile. In the next field head left of centre passing the outside corner of a fenced field on the right and go through a large gate directly ahead. Walk ahead again, but keep a little more to the left to reach a stile in the far left-hand corner which leads onto a path. Turn right and follow the path for a little over 100 yards before turning left through a gate into a small field. Walk ahead to a stile in the corner and ahead again to pass through a gap in the far hedge. Continue ahead and in the next corner bear left with the wall to a farm. Adjacent to the farmhouse, turn right through a gate, bear left past the house and follow the track to the road. Turn right and follow the road down to Graianrhyd to complete the walk.

Bodidris Hall

Southern Clwydians from Craig-fechan

Distance: *6¹/₂ or 7³/₄ miles*

An enjoyable walk using old drovers' roads to gain the Clwydian ridge, followed by a section of the Offa's Dyke Path. The walk is centred on the little known village of Graig-fechan with its excellent pub, 'The Three Pigeons'.

Start: Begin the walk at the 'Three Pigeons Inn' in the little village of Craig-fechan where there is a car park and an information board. This lies about 2 miles southeast of Ruthin on the B5429. *Grid ref: 147 544 (Landranger 116, Explorer 256).*

The walk

1. Turn right along the lane passing the 'Three Pigeons Inn' and take the signed bridleway on the left beside the stream. Almost immediately, bear left off the main track onto a narrower footpath which rises to a second track. Turn left and follow the track past a house on the left. Continue ahead on the footpath through woods to pass a second house on the left. Cross the stile just after the house and continue on the path ahead through the woods.

In about 300 yards with a small field immediately ahead, bear right for about 15 yards to a path junction. Here you have a choice. For a longer and more strenuous walk continue from point **2**.

For a shorter walk turn sharp right onto a waymarked footpath which climbs up through the trees. At the top of the rise keep straight ahead as waymarked and drop to a fence. Turn

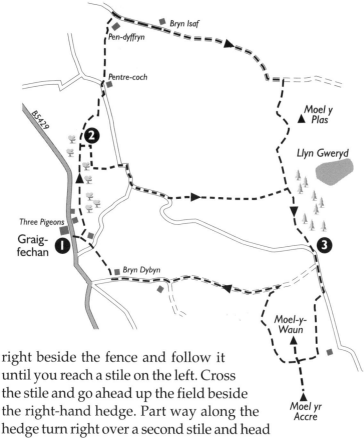

right beside the fence and follow it
until you reach a stile on the left. Cross
the stile and go ahead up the field beside
the right-hand hedge. Part way along the
hedge turn right over a second stile and head
left up the field to a stile in the top corner just before a farm
which leads into a lane. Turn right along the lane and at a fork
with the farm to the right keep ahead (left) signed 'Llanarmon
yn Iâl 5'.

Follow the lane for about 450 yards where it bears right over
a stone bridge. Take either the path immediately before the bridge
on the left which rises through an attractive little valley, bracken
covered on its left side to join the Offa's Dyke Path near conifers
on the skyline, or take the field path through the gate on the left
after the bridge. This passes through a number of fields on the
right-hand side of the stream to a stile almost at the head of the

valley. Cross the stile and walk beside the fence to the top of the rise with a mast ahead. Bear half-right to join the Offa's Dyke Path where a line of power cables start.

Which ever option you take turn right and follow Offa's Dyke Path to the road. Continue from Point **3**.

2. For the longer walk, bear left along the edge of the woods with a small field to the left. Stay on this path beside the fence until your way is blocked by a wooden fence/stile in the corner of the wood. Cross the fence/stile and walk ahead to eventually reach a gate with a house beyond and a stile on the right. Don't go through the gate, instead, turn right over the stile and bear left along the hedge to a second stile hidden down in the lower corner of the field which leads into the lane at the hamlet of Pentre-côch.

Turn left along the lane past the cottages gathered around the stream and where the lane curves left, take the signed footpath on the right adjacent to the gate of 'Plas-tirion'. Go into fields by a stone stile and turn left to pass behind the house. In the corner pass through a gateway into the next field and walk with the hedge on the right and a small lake over to the left. In the next field head for the railings which enclose the garden of the large house ahead ('Pen-dyffryn') and keep left around the garden to a stile on the right which leads down onto the access track. Turn right for a few yards then bear left over a footbridge immediately before stone pillars. Walk up to a stile on the left then pass farm buildings to a gate into the lane. Turn right up the lane.

Higher up (after 'Bryn Isaf' on the left) the lane becomes an unsurfaced bridleway, one of many green lanes which probably originated as a drovers' route through the hills to markets in England centuries ago.

Continue the steady climb for about ¾ mile until the track swings left up to the pass between Moel Llech to the north and Moel y Plâs to the south.

Offa's Dyke Path crosses the pass here having traversed the length of the Clwydian Range; one of the finest section of the route.

Turn right over the stile and follow the signed ODP up onto the shoulder of Moel y Plas. At the top of the rise follow the path ahead through the heather and beside the fence until a stile leads into grazing fields. Turn right for about 35 yards, then bear left down a sloping field.

Ahead in clear conditions you have broad views to Cyrn-y-Brain and the hills of Llantysilio Mountain crossed by the famous Horseshoe Pass. Out to the southwest lie the higher summits of the Berwyn mountains beyond the Dee valley.

At the bottom of the slope cross the stile and continue ahead beside woods on the left to eventually reach a lane.

3. Go straight ahead up the rising lane and at the top turn right over a stile into fields. Walk ahead to reach the grass covered remains of an old wall. Follow this as it curves left to contour the hillside. After about 300 yards you reach the outside corner of a

Following Offa's Dyke Path on the shoulder of Moel y Plâs

fence; keep ahead beside the fence to a stile in the corner of the field. Climb the stile and rise (straight ahead) through the centre of an open field to a stile on the skyline.

Access to both Moel y Waun and Moel yr Accre is by short footpaths on the right and left. A return should be made to this point to continue.

Beyond the stile follow a descending footpath which swings half-right into grazing fields. Keep bearing right in this field to join a farm track which runs beside the fence. Follow this track to a stile in the fence on the left just before a small group of trees. Turn left over the stile and walk down the field to the far right corner where two gates near sheep pens lead onto another farm track. Turn left down the track.

In about ½ mile keep right where the track forks and right again by a cottage ('Pen-y-Bryn Farm') lower down. Follow the descending lane (which is now surfaced) past a small farm on the right ('Ty Coch') and immediately after the next bungalow on the right ('Bryn Dibyn') take the signed footpath on the right into fields. Cut diagonally through the field to a stile and footbridge in the opposite corner. Bear half-left in the following field to a stile which leads between gardens. Turn right down the drive to a narrow lane.

Turn right then immediately left into an access road between houses ('Bronallt' and 'Glandwr'). Follow the road until you pass bungalows down to the left (about 250 yards). Immediately after this, the road swings sharp right and there are two limestone rocks on the right. Go ahead on the bend off the road onto an unsurfaced track. In about 50 yards take the path on the left and retrace the outward route to complete the walk.

Llandegla &
Llyn Cyfynwy

Distance: *6 miles*

Pleasant walking through farmland on part of the Offa's Dyke Path with a gentle climb onto the Llandegla Moors and the broad open views to be enjoyed from Llyn Cyfynwy.

Note: It may be difficult to cross the stream near Pen-y-Bryn farm towards the end of the walk in very wet conditions.

Start: There is a small car park situated between the church and Post Office in the village of Llandegla.
Grid ref: 196 524 (Landranger 116 & 117, Explorer 256).

Llandegla is a small quiet village situated off the main traffic routes in the broad basin-shaped valley where the infant Afon Alyn takes its first faltering steps. But things were not always so quiet here; for centuries a nearby holy well, famous for its ability to cure epilepsy or 'falling sickness' as it was known, attracted visitors from miles around and was noted by Thomas Pennant who passed this way in the late eighteenth century. The well is reputed to be the second oldest healing well in Britain.

The most notable building in the village is the church, rebuilt in the nineteenth century and containing an unusual fifteenth century brass chandelier similar to the one at nearby Llanarmon-yn-Iâl.

During the Middle Ages Llandegla lay in the commote of Iâl (pronounced 'yale') thought to have been controlled from a motte and bailey castle built by Owain Gwynedd in 1149. This controlled entry into the valuable lands of the Vale of Clwyd and is situated at the head

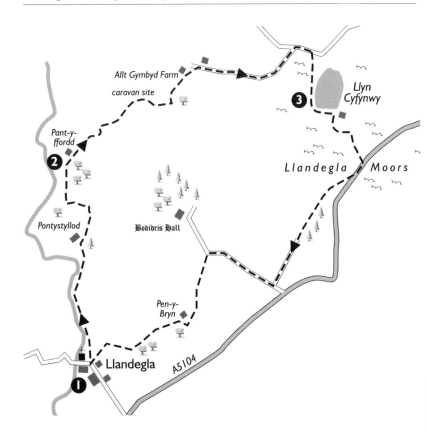

of the Nant-y-Glyn Pass where its earthworks can be seen today. Known as Tomen-y-Rhodwydd, it was attacked and burnt by Iowerth Goch ap Maredudd of Powys but later restored in the reign of King John.

The walk

1. Take the Offa's Dyke Path beside the church (with 'The Old Rectory' on the right) where a track leads into fields. Follow the signed footpath ahead with the infant meandering Afon Alyn close by on the left. At a footbridge don't cross the river, instead turn right over the adjacent stile. Walk directly through the following large field looking for a stile beyond a small stone footbridge on the right at the far end of the field. Keep left along the field edge to a second stile and beyond turn right up to the lane.

Walk left along the lane towards 'Pontystyllod' farm and just before the farm buildings, take the signed path into woods on the right. After a short stretch in the trees enter fields again keeping ahead to a stile in the upper fence. Keep ahead again with low limestone outcrops and a tree-topped bank on the left until there is a gap in the bank. Turn left through the gap and cross a small field to a stile to reach a track. The track soon curves round right towards a house with tennis courts. Almost as soon as this comes into view look for a gate down to the left. Go through the gate following the fence on the left to a second gate. Keep left with the fence again to a stile and drop to a track. Turn left and follow the track towards a farm (Pant-y-ffordd).

Looking down into the upper Alyn valley

2. Just before the farm outbuildings where the track swings left, take the signed bridleway through a gate on the right. Pass the farm and follow the bridleway as it begins a gradual climb out of the Alyn valley. Higher up, follow the signed bridleway right at a fingerpost where the grass track continues ahead contouring rather than climbing. At the top of the field a gate leads onto an enclosed path bordered by a broken wall on the left. At a caravan site keep right and continue to eventually reach a lane near the caravan site entrance ('Allt Gymbyd Farm').

Turn right and follow the lane for almost ³/₄ mile.

At a T junction turn right and in 100 yards or so a stile on the right (opposite a bridleway which joins the lane from the left) marks a permissive footpath which skirts a wet marshy area before rising leftwards a short distance to Llyn Cyfynwy. Alternatively, a right of way also leads up to the lake but the path is in a poorer condition. This can be reached by continuing along the lane (150 yards) to a signed footpath on the right on the bend (partly hidden at the time of writing). Go over the stile and walk straight up through the heather beside a crumbling stone wall to the shore of the lake.

The open nature of the moors allows wide views back towards the sweeping green slopes of the Clwydian Range, from Moel yr Accre to Moel Famau. To the north the quarrying at Graig and Graianrhyd scars an otherwise pastoral landscape.

Llyn Cyfynwy sits in a small hollow just below the highest point on the moors and will often be ringed by fishermen. On the walk down to the road you will see how a lack of burning the heather is allowing bracken, scrub and birch to encroach on what used to be an unbroken purple carpet in August and September

3. The path goes right (anticlockwise) around the lake to pass near a chalet on the far side. From here turn right down the access track away from the lake and down to the road (A5104). Turn right along the road for about 75 yards before bearing right onto a signed footpath. The right of way follows a track at first before bearing left over a stile just before a cattle grid and gate. A second stile leads into fields and the path continues ahead with the fence on the left.

The pyramidal hill ahead is Moel Morfydd, one of the hills on the sweeping Llantysilio ridge.

After passing woods on the left a farm track is reached. Keep straight ahead ignoring the right fork. At the end of the track turn right at a T junction signed to 'Bodidris Hall'. Follow the lane for almost ½ mile and where it turns sharp right up towards the Hall, go left through a gate and cut through a large open field in the direction of a large farm (Pen-y-Bryn). Go through a gate and walk below small limestone crags on the left with the farm still ahead and aim for a stile to the left of the buildings. Bear right after the stile to the access track and head right up towards the house.

Don't follow the track as it curves right into the yard, instead continue ahead following arrows, then, at the top of a bank turn left down to a stile. After the stile, zig-zag down the bank and turn left to cross a stream by a footbridge to a stile on the far bank. Walk straight through the following fields passing close to a small lake on the right and cross a stream. In the next field keep close to woods on the left for about 200 yards then bear half-right through the centre of the field (aim to the right of houses) to a stile which leads onto a farm road. Turn left and follow the road to Llandegla to complete the walk.

Mara Books www.marabooks.co.uk

MARA BOOKS publish a range of walking books for Cheshire and North Wales and have the following list to date.

North Wales

Circular Walks in the Conwy Valley

ISBN 0 9522409 7 1. A collection of 18 circular walks which explore the varied scenery of this beautiful valley from the Great Orme to Betws-y-Coed.

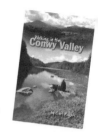

A pocket guide to Snowdon

ISBN 1 902512 04 9. A guide to all Snowdon's recognised routes of ascent, from the six 'Classic Paths' to the many lesser known and less frequented routes.

Walking in Snowdonia Volume 1

ISBN 1 902512 06 5. A series of circular walks exploring the beautiful and dramatic valleys in the northern half of the Snowdonia National Park.

Coastal Walks around Anglesey Volume 1

ISBN 0 9522409 6 3. A collection of 15 walks which explore the varied scenery of Anglesey's beautiful coastline.

Coastal Walks around Anglesey Volume 2

ISBN 0 9522409 5 5. A companion volume to the above book, outlining 15 new walks spread around Anglesey's fascinating and beautiful coastline.

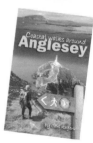

Walking the Isle of Anglesey Coastal Path
ISBN 1 902512 13 8. The official guide for the Isle of Anglesey Coastal Path. Full colour in English and Welsh.

Walking on the Lleyn Peninsula
ISBN 1 902512 00 6. A collection of 16 circular walks which explore the wild and beautiful coastline and hills of the Lleyn Peninsula.

Walking in the Vale of Clwyd and Denbigh Moors
ISBN 1 902512 15 4. A collection of circular walks exploring the undiscovered country between the Clwydian Range and the Conwy Valley.

The Mountain Men
ISBN 1 902512 11 1. This book tells the story of the pioneer rock climbers in Snowdonia in the closing decades of the nineteenth century until the outbreak of World War I.

Cheshire

Circular Walks along the Sandstone Trail
ISBN 1 902512 10 3. The Sandstone Trail is Cheshire's best known and most popular walking route. This book gives a complete route description along with 12 circular walks covering the entire trail.

A Walker's Guide to the Wirral Shore Way

ISBN 1 902512 05 7. A linear walk of 23 miles following the old coastline between Chester and Hoylake.

Circular Walks along the Gritstone Trail and Mow Cop Trail

ISBN 0 9522409 4 7. A route which follows Cheshire's eastern border along the edge of the Peak District. Following the same format as the Sandstone Trail book—a full description for both trails is combined with 12 circular walks.

Circular Walks in Wirral

ISBN 1 902512 02 2. A collection of 15 circular walks in the coast and countryside of Wirral.

Published by North Eye Books

www.northerneyebooks.co.uk

Walks in Mysterious Cheshire and Wirral

ISBN 0 9553557 0 2. A collection of 14 circular walks exploring Cheshire's historic landscape.